Fool's Gold

The Life and Legacy of Vancouver's
Official Town Fool

JESSE DONALDSON

Anvil Press • Vancouver

Anvil Press Publishers Inc.
PO Box 3008, Station Terminal
Vancouver, BC V6B 3X5 Canada
anvilpress.com

Library and Archives Canada Cataloguing in Publication

Title: Fool's gold : the life and legacy of Vancouver's town fool / by Jesse Donaldson.
Names: Donaldson, Jesse, 1982- author.
Description: First edition. | Series statement: 49.2 : tales from the offbeat ; #2
Identifiers: Canadiana 20200362038 | ISBN 9781772141467 (softcover)
Subjects: LCSH: Foikis, Joachim. | LCSH: Fools and jesters—British Columbia—Vancouver—Biography. |
  LCSH: Vancouver (B.C.)—Biography. | LCGFT: Biographies.
Classification: LCC FC3847.26.F64 D66 2020 | DDC 971.1/3304092—dc23

Book design by Clint Hutzulak/Rayola.com
Author photo by Albert Nicholas Photography
Represented in Canada by Publishers Group Canada
Distributed by Raincoast Books

The publisher gratefully acknowledges the financial assistance of the Canada Council for the Arts, the Canada Book Fund, and the Province of British Columbia through the BC Arts Council and the Book Publishing Tax Credit.

Printed and bound in Canada

CONTENTS

Introduction   5

APRIL FOOL'S DAY   11

FOLLY OF YOUTH   15
1: Ship of Fools   17
2: End of the World   93
3: Epiphany   33
4: Valentine's Day   67

"Kim Foikis Is A Man Who Radiates Life"   41

A FOOL AND HIS MONEY   45
5: The Grant   77
6: Fool on the Hill   25
7: Peter and Pan   51
8: Drum and Colours   101
9: Great Fall (Part One)   83

FOOL'S PARADISE   91
    10: Magic Mountain   57
    11: "Meaningful Work"   97
    12: Great Fall (Part Two)   47

"Fools Rush In"   109

    Acknowledgments   115
    Notes   117
    About the Author   125

INTRODUCTION

There's a very good chance I'm misrepresenting Kim Foikis. But as far as I can tell, that would be okay with him.

"How can you misrepresent me?" he once asked film director Tom Shandel, at the height of his popularity. "I'm a bouncing ball. Whatever you do with me, it's according to your own folly. You've used me in your own fashion."

Like many people, I was fascinated by the man from the moment I first read about him; his wit, his commitment, his obvious intelligence, and the fact that he seemed impervious to the scorn and derision that inevitably came his way. But transforming a small collection of magazine features, newspaper interviews, and personal anecdotes into anything approaching a book proved to be something of a fool's errand. Even with the help of half a dozen surviving friends and acquaintances (bless them all), there are vast swathes of his life that remain a mystery, many key motivations that remain unknown. Attempts to locate surviving relatives — in particular, his son Martin, last documented working at York University in 1999 — proved fruitless. His daughter hadn't spoken to him since the mid-1970s. The memories of friends had become foggy, and some pieces of information were infuriatingly contradictory.

Which, as far as I can tell, would probably be okay with him, too.

"I want to be a mythic character," he told Shandel. "And I want to create a legend — a Vancouver legend."

The reasons for that, he said, were because myths present fundamental truths in a simpler form. They're able to distill complicated information down to a series of images — often universal ones. And so, he did what he could to create those images. But he didn't wait for his audience to come to him. Instead, he took it to the streets. There was a nursery rhyme he often quoted:

"The cock doth crow,
to let you know,
That if you're wise,
'Tis time to rise."

It was his mission, he said, to create joy and confusion. To upend things. To be a reflection of the folly he saw in the world. But more than that, he wanted to wake people up. And so, the result is a book that's intended to be a reflection of the man — as much a work of nonfiction as it is a work of folly, a book intended to be as joyful as it is confusing. You can certainly read it the traditional way if that's what you'd prefer — the chapters are still properly numbered. Or you could join Kim and me on a voyage of whimsy, travelling as he did, this way and that, a bouncing ball that moved back and forth between red and blue, heaven and hell, community and isolation, celebrity and poverty, study and frolic, fatherhood and abandonment, life and death.

As the Turkish philosopher and fool Mulla Nasrudin would say: "I am upside-down in this world." So please — join us. Upend yourself. And let Kim Foikis wake you up. More than anything else, I think that would probably be okay with him.

Or maybe that's just a reflection of my own folly.

Jesse Donaldson
November 2020

"When I was a little boy
I had but little wit;
'Tis a long time ago,
And I have no more yet;
Nor ever ever shall
Until that I die,
For the longer I live
The more fool am I."

— **Excerpt from *Mother Goose's Melody*, 1817**

"What place can there be for a minstrel now,
against these ghastly times?
For one who would sing to a light guitar,
his picaroonish rhymes.
When the pain and filth of war go on
and we lack for bread.
Oh, the Dark Fool is loose in the world.
And the Fool of Joy is dead."

— Tom MacInnes, 1918

APRIL FOOL'S DAY

April 1, 1968

It was April Fool's Day, and Joachim Foikis was about to turn the city upside down.

The red and blue of his homemade uniform shone under the pop of flashbulbs as reporters and photographers formed a tight scrum around him, and the jangle of the bells on his cap made the foyer of Vancouver's City Hall — normally a place dripping with righteous self-importance — feel more like a carnival sideshow. In one hand, he carried a sceptre adorned with a jester's head.

In the other was a cheque for $3,500.

Diligently, he answered question after shouted question, his voice soft, his responses peppered with quotes from Socrates, Shakespeare, Mother Goose. Occasionally he paused to click his heels, to jump for joy, to thumb his nose at Mayor Tom Campbell.

"Now I can give my whole time to my job," he grinned, "to live joyfully for nothing, and to spread joy and confusion."

When a reporter asked how he was adjusting to his newfound celebrity, Foikis merely shrugged.

"The biggest fools always get lots of publicity."

He was thirty-six years old. Tall. Soft-spoken, with an unmistakable German accent. His face didn't look like the type that took easily to smiling, but he was generally cheerful; and his eyes, peering out from behind a pair of square-framed glasses, were said to "radiate life" and mischief by those who knew him.

Just a year earlier, he had been a self-described "bookworm" living a quiet life in a bungalow on West Fifteenth Avenue in Kitsilano. A husband and father of two. An introvert. A former social worker with two university degrees — one in theology and the other in economics — who had only six weeks to go before he graduated with a third, in library sciences, from the University of British Columbia.

But then he'd seen an angel.

"[T]he angel appeared and whispered in my ear," he later explained, "and told me to take up the bauble."

And take it up he had. Shortly after his vision, Joachim Foikis had revived a tradition unseen for centuries and declared himself Vancouver's official town fool. Beginning in the spring of 1967, dressed in his traditional red-and-blue fool's motley, he had set up shop on the steps of the city courthouse, where he spent two to three hours each day dispensing philosophy to adults and nursery rhymes to children. He had wandered the streets talking to passers-by with his bauble in hand — the iconic jester-headed staff that served as the source of the Fool's power, a constant reminder that no one was above mockery — least of all the fool himself.

"Are you a man?" he would ask the downtown business elite, as they hurried from place to place, or looked up, startled, from their newspapers. "Or a fool?"

But now, Joachim Foikis was more than just a fool — he was a fool with the blessing of the federal government. The cheque in his hand was a grant from the Canada Council for the Arts, and for the next year, it would allow him to make folly his full-time job.

"Dressed in traditional fool's motley, he has nursery rhymes for children and metaphysical riddles for adults," read the council's press release. "To many, he is making a serious contribution to the self-awareness of the entire community."

Meanwhile, up in his office, far from the hubbub, Mayor Campbell seethed.

"When I read about it this morning, I saw red," he griped to a *Vancouver Sun* reporter. "An old-age pensioner, who's worked all his life for his country, gets $1,200 a year. Here's a fellow who refuses to work and they give him a $3,500 young-age pension. Couldn't we use it for public housing for senior citizens, retarded children, pensioners, deserving students?"

"I do not mock thee, but by thee am mocked," Foikis retorted, quoting William Blake. "Thou call'st me madman, but I call thee blockhead."

After just ten minutes of questions, he headed for the door, pausing only briefly outside to chat with a CBC camera crew. There was no time to waste. His was more than a vocation — it was a calling. He would later tell a friend that he felt "touched," compelled into action by something larger than himself.

"I want to revive the Fool of Joy," he told reporters. "I want all the world to be a stage — and get every other fool to laugh in the face of death."

In the years ahead, he would do exactly that. He would make it his mission to transform himself into a living work of performance art, a fool that the country took much delight in, amusing children and irritating magistrates from coast to coast. One charged with spreading the gospel of Mother Goose, promulgating a unique worldview forged in the ashes of the Second World War and honed through a decade of study, one which held a funhouse mirror up to the topsy-turvy world of the 1960s. He would become a figure who ferreted out folly wherever it could be found — on the sidewalks, in the boardrooms, and in the halls of power. It was a mission that would take him across the country and back, bringing him to international prominence, and seeing him featured in the pages of the *Vancouver Sun*, *The Globe and Mail*, *Maclean's*, *The New York Times*, and the *Encyclopædia Britannica*. It would find him hosting impromptu dance parties in the streets — from the Granville strip to the Downtown Eastside to downtown Toronto — or speaking at universities, colleges, and even the prestigious Esalen Institute.

It would also cost him his marriage, his children, his public profile — and in the eyes of some — his sanity. It would leave him homeless and land him in court more than once. So, who was Joachim Foikis? Mystic? Freeloader? Genius? Madman? Hero? Blockhead? Or truth-seeker on a lifelong search for meaning, one set against the backdrop of a world plagued by folly — a life that ended forty years after that fateful vision, in a fashion that was equal parts comic, tragic, and poetic. Although his legacy would be largely forgotten in the ensuing years, he would, in a small way, for a short time, turn the city — and the world — upside down, with a song in his heart and a drum in his hand.

But all of that was yet to come. For today was April Fool's Day. And Joachim Foikis had work to do.

FOLLY OF YOUTH

"I'm a Mother Goose Witness. Jehovah's Witnesses say the world is coming to an end tomorrow. I say the world is just beginning — maybe today."

— Joachim Foikis, *Coshocton Tribune*, November 20, 1968

1.

SHIP OF FOOLS

"When that I was and a little tiny boy,
With hey, ho, the wind and the rain,
A foolish thing was but a toy,
For the rain it raineth every day."

— Feste, *Twelfth Night*

THE UPPER SILESIA REGION where Joachim Foikis was born had always been something of a fool's paradise.

"The last fools," he once told a reporter, died out "near the village where I was born."

For centuries, the courts of Germany and Poland had been a fertile breeding ground for famous fools; there, the tradition was stronger and carried on longer than anywhere else in Europe, featuring notable characters, real and folkloric — the German Till Eulenspiegel (invented in the 1300s and said to favour pranks involving his own faeces) and the Polish Stańczyk both appeared in poems, paintings, and plays well after the rest of Europe's fools had disappeared.

Of course, the fool tradition predated its appearance in Europe by thousands of years. The term itself came from the Latin *follis* (roughly translating to "bag of wind"), and the ideology (if it could be described as such) had its roots in cynic philosophy — including disdain for material wealth, rejection of social mores, and the use of one's own body as a tool for social comment. As far back as ancient Greece, Diogenes of Sinope (one of the founders of Cynicism) had generated storms of controversy when he settled in Athens with a self-imposed mission to challenge Greek cultural norms. The son of a banker, Diogenes seems to have had an epiphany of sorts, where-after he took a stand against the family business by defacing local currency — an act for which he was exiled from Sinope and stripped of all of his material possessions. Undeterred, he moved to Athens to live a life of austerity, taking up residence inside a large ceramic jar in the city's marketplace, where he immediately began ruffling feathers. One of his most famous stunts involved wandering the city square with a lamp in broad daylight, claiming to be involved in the endless search for an honest man. He regularly mocked the great thinkers and politicians of his day; after reading Plato's dialogue "Statesmen," which described men as "featherless bipeds," Diogenes plucked a chicken and brought it to the famed philosopher's Academy, declaring "Behold! I've brought you a man!" It has been reported that once he even criticized Alexander the Great; when the general recognized Diogenes on the streets of Corinth and asked if he could do any favour for the noted philosopher, Diogenes simply asked him to "stand out of my sunlight."

In the centuries that followed, the fool tradition spread all over the world, from China, to Europe, to the Middle East. Some were simple entertainers or travelling minstrels. Others found themselves on the civic payroll; many German cities employed professional fools year-round for use at country fairs and celebrations, each with a spe-cific specialty — including the "trick player" and the "saying sayer." It seems to have been an exclusively male profession; no female fools have been recorded anywhere in the Western world. But the fool's function wasn't simply to amuse. Like in the days of Diogenes, the goal was instead to illuminate, to be a funhouse mirror held up to society — one that ridiculed its conventions, its hang-ups, and its institutions. Even the scatologically-inclined Till Eulenspiegel served this purpose; his name was likely a combination of the German words for "owl" — implying wisdom — and "mirror" (or according to others, simply a pun on the Low German phrase "wipe-ass"). For some, a life of speaking truth to power was their ticket to fame and fortune; the antics of Abū Nuwās of Baghdad gained him a royal appointment in the court of Caliph Harun al-Rashid. When Pubmann, court jester to Frederick I of Prussia died, the king insisted his fool be buried in a place of honour, in the centre of a church — despite the fact that the clergy (who he regularly taunted) had denied him the privilege on the grounds of sacrilege.

"Pubmann was a preacher of truth and didn't even spare me," Frederick argued. "Consequently, he deserves to be buried in the center of the church, a place where nothing but the pure truth should be preached."

During the thirteenth century, Sufi fool Mulla Nasrudin served as vizier in the court of Kaykaus II and became known the world over for his antics, which brought together political commentary and philosophy. As his legend grew, new stories and anecdotes were added to the canon; and fact merged with fiction, leading to the development of a diverse set of Nasrudin-type characters all over the world — from Turkey, to Romania, to China, to Greece, to India.

"Some people say that, whilst uttering what seemed madness," an author wrote, in the late 1880s, "he was, in reality, divinely inspired, and that it was not madness but wisdom that he uttered."

Nasrudin had a simpler way of describing his worldview.

"I am," he said, "upside down in this world."

During the Renaissance, the fool was a regular fixture in courts across Europe, and some, like Will Sommers (fool to Henry VIII), and Jeffrey Hudson (Charles I), had become household names for espousing their topsy-turvy perspective. But folly wasn't always the safest occupation; in the early 1600s, Archibald Armstrong (fool to James VI of Scotland), was thrown out of the royal entourage for ruffling too many feathers. Even Sommers was once threatened with death after Henry caught him referring to the future Queen Elizabeth I as a "bastard." But the Protestant Reformation heralded the end of the fool's days in court; with Charles II's ascension to the English throne in the mid-1600s, the practice was discontinued.

"[T]he fool went out as the Puritans came in," Joachim Foikis would later note. "They couldn't bear to have their prejudices pricked."

By the early 1700s, the fool had all but vanished from Europe, with one notable exception: Poland. There, Stańczyk experienced a renaissance that lasted well into the nineteenth century. The character's antics had always been political, but by the 1800s, he was appearing in plays and paintings as an overt symbol of Poland's struggle for independence from Russian occupation. The character reached the height of his prominence in Stanisław Wyspiański's influential 1901 play *The Wedding*, where the fool exhorted the main character to "stir the nation" to fight for its freedom.

The question of Polish sovereignty had been largely settled by the time Joachim Foikis was born on August 11, 1931, and Stańczyk — like all the previous fools save Till Eulenspiegel — had long since vanished from art and literature. At birth, his surname was spelled "Fojkis", meaning "Big Fish" — though he would later change the spelling — and he spent his first years in Siemianowice, a small Polish village near Auschwitz. Originally, the family hailed from the Greek province of Phocis — once said to have been home to the Oracle of Delphi. Details of his early life are scant, but his upbringing wasn't a pleasant one; some of it, he later noted, was spent in a children's home. He rarely mentioned his father in interviews, except to say that he was "a mayor." The surname Fojkis does indeed appear on regional election paperwork, listed as a "burgomaster" (mayor) in 1931, the same year young Joachim was born. At the same time, there was a famous politician in the area who shared the same last name — Walenty Fojkis, a celebrated commander during the Silesian Uprisings, and later an MP and head of a commune in Siemianowice itself. According to surviving records, the surname was an uncommon one; in the region around Siemianowice, there is only one recorded birth — that of Franciszek Fojkis in 1918, to parents Jan and Zofia. Just three students are listed in the 1926 Polish Declarations of Admiration and Friendship for the United States, a document signed by virtually every schoolchild in Poland. Whether Walenty Fojkis and Joachim's father are the same man is difficult to determine, but given the rarity of the last name, some form of familial relationship — extended or otherwise — seems likely. While the Silesian Uprisings that led to Walenty Fojkis' fame had ended by the early 1930s, the region wasn't exactly peaceful; the League of Nations had advocated for Poland's independence, but tensions and violence continued to flare up between Polish citizens and the German minority. There was also plenty of tension at home, and at the age of four, Foikis' parents divorced, his mother moving the family to Berlin, where she opened a toy shop.

By the dawn of the Third Reich, Berlin's cabaret comedians had taken up the mantle of the fools of old, using song, satire, and bawdy humour to skewer the politicians and institutions of the day; the evening after Kristallnacht, performer Weiß Ferdl took the stage draped in jewellery, saying "Did you think I'd slept through crystal night?" However, the totalitarian ethos of the Nazi government had little patience for even the most minor dissent — something cabaret comedian Werner Finck discovered after his antics landed him in a concentration camp. For young men like Joachim Foikis, the realities of wartime Germany weren't immediately clear. He spent the next several years attending school and church, and in 1941 he, like most men his age, joined the Hitler Youth — although he quickly became disillusioned.

"One day I came home from school and the SS were throwing everything out of the big apartments of Jews," he later said. "Like in the movie *Schindler's List*, the street was lined with SS trucks. I asked, 'Where are you taking them?'"

The deportees, he discovered, were being sent to a work camp north of Berlin. This development didn't sit well with the twelve-year-old Foikis, and in short order, his discomfort turned to revulsion; while on a trip to Poland, he heard the first whispered rumours about the horrors of Auschwitz. After only two years, he hung up his uniform forever — along with what remained of his faith.

"That's when I stopped saying 'Heil Hitler' and dropped out of Hitler Youth and the Roman Catholic Church," he explained.

As the war escalated, the world around him seemed to descend further into madness with each passing day. Almost 25,000 allied troops had landed at Normandy and were said to be making their way toward Berlin. Bombs dropped from British, French, and Soviet airplanes had wiped entire neighbourhoods off the map, killing thousands; and leaving hundreds of thousands homeless. Fire had consumed dozens of childhood landmarks. Many of his friends — older by two years and thus drafted — now found themselves imprisoned in Soviet POW camps. But despite the chaos, Foikis remained in the city, his passion for learning nurtured by a handful of teachers and mentors.

"My high school in Berlin was idealistic, mystical, humanitarian," he explained. "My teacher sent me out on the road to truth rather than the road to success. I have always followed that road."

Mysticism was a concept Foikis would revisit time and again throughout his life. Although his disdain for religion would persist — he later described Protestantism as "a combination of greed and social climbing" — he quickly discovered a new sort of gospel: books. And soon enough, his faltering Catholicism was replaced by a different sort of spirituality — one informed by some unlikely sources.

"I recall enjoying *Grimms' Fairy Tales*," he later noted, "because, on the wings of the imagination, I was lifted into a world of wonder and enchantment, which seemed more real than the insane social machine around me."

And on the day the war ended, his developing spiritual philosophy suddenly expanded to include something else: on May 8, 1945, while standing amongst the smoking ruins of Berlin, the thirteen-year-old Foikis had his first vision.

"[O]n this day everything was in ruins," he recalled. "It seemed that I saw the whole world transfigured. On that one day there was total anarchy and total peace."

Over the next several years, Berlin continued its transformation. Tensions rose as the city was carved into three different sections — each under the control of a different Allied power. All railroads into West Berlin were blocked. All emigration from communist East Berlin was banned, and as the Cold War intensified, the streets quickly became home to more spies than any other city on the planet. Thanks to his studious nature and the support of his teachers, Foikis managed to thrive in West Berlin, finishing high school and, sometime between 1948 and 1951, enrolling at the newly established Free University of Berlin. The university itself was only a few years old, created after a massive protest in 1947, when students from communist-controlled East Berlin demanded an institution free from government influence. It's unclear whether Joachim Foikis paid his own way or received a scholarship; however, given his academic aptitude and the encouragement of his professors, it seems reasonable to assume the latter. And during the four years he spent on campus earning a degree in economics, he would have been exposed to a much more cosmopolitan world than he was used to. By 1949, the school was home to almost 5,000 people, and owing to the part they had played in its formation, students exercised a greater degree of control than in virtually any other European university.

No accounts survive of Foikis' time in university. As is the case with much of his life, information on the years between 1948 and 1955 is spotty. He never discussed it in interviews, and his remaining friends don't remember hearing any details or anecdotes about the period. Only a few things are clear: first, he graduated with a degree in economics sometime between 1952 and 1955; second, he paid his father a visit in 1953, after which he never spoke to him again; and lastly, Joachim Foikis decided it was time for a change.

Perhaps it was wanderlust. Perhaps it was curiosity. Perhaps it was another of his visions. Or perhaps walking away from his friends, his family, and his homeland was simply the folly of youth. In any event, he was soon to arrive in a far-off place with a very different sort of fool tradition — one where the tricksters of folklore didn't just hold a mirror up to society, but actively interfered with it. It was a journey that would end in lovers meeting. The destination on his plane ticket read Toronto, Canada, but this wouldn't be the end of his wanderings.

No, Joachim Foikis was bound for the end of the world.

6.

FOOL ON THE HILL

"Foolery, sir, does walk about the orb like the sun; it shines everywhere."

— Feste, *Twelfth Night*

IT WAS THE MIDDLE OF 1968, and Joachim Foikis was at the height of his powers.

"The world is governed by folly," he declared to a national audience in the pages of *The Globe and Mail*. "The world is in the same situation as Humpty Dumpty. It has fallen apart. All the king's horses and all the king's men couldn't put Humpty Dumpty together again."

As of January, *The Globe and Mail*'s Richard Needham had nominated him as Canada's unofficial Man of the Year. In March, he was invited to lecture at a six-week CBC-sponsored symposium at York University entitled: "Images, Idiots, and Idols." In May, he was featured in *The New York Times*, and their wire service sent the profile to American newspapers from Baltimore to Montana. Jack Mangles,

owner of the Abbotsford Hotel on Hastings Street, offered to pad
out Foikis' grant money with an additional $4,000 from his own
pocket — an offer Foikis adamantly refused.

"I do not believe there should be profit in foolery," he told a
reporter.

In April, he and his family attended a "be-in" at Stanley Park.
Shortly after that, he hopped a train and returned to Ontario for the
second time that year, wearing his cap and bells for the entirety of the
multi-day journey. The publicity generated by Needham's "Save the
Fool" campaign had raised enough money and awareness for a three-
week speaking tour; and over the course of the month, Foikis spoke
at a dozen venues, including a church in London, a high school in
Scarborough, and Guelph's annual Spring Festival.

"In some of the smaller towns, the people would look away when
they saw me," he laughed. "They didn't want to embarrass me. They
thought I was nuts."

His engagements usually took the form of an informal Q&A —
often with Foikis wandering the room — and sometimes led to interesting tête-à-têtes with students; at Woburn Collegiate Institute in
Scarborough, a teenage boy questioned the usefulness of being a
philosopher who played the fool, to which Foikis shrugged, reply-
ing: "I'm laughing at you." And on either end of his trip, he visited
Toronto, making a series of lunchtime speeches outside of City Hall.

"Canada may be the land of milk and honey, but it needs spirit,"
he told the crowd. "I want to help people lose some of their psychic
constipation."

These speeches drew large crowds, with several Toronto residents
asking if they could become apprentices ("[P]lease don't forget," Foikis told them, "I'm just an apprentice"). But privately, as Foikis
confided to Richard Needham — who was by now as much a friend
as he was a journalist — he was less interested in giving speeches than
he was in creating "happenings."

"The less I analyze the position of fool and other things, the better. The challenge really lies in creating a stage around me on which individuals can experience a moment of truth — that is, they should be free to put on the persona or mask which is closest to their heart's desire."

Over the course of his trip, he put this into practice several times; after one of his lunchtime speeches, he crashed a meeting of city council to put his hat onto Mayor William Dennison. Infuriated, Dennison had him removed from chambers, refusing to even shake Foikis' hand ("He doesn't have much imagination," Foikis said). At the end of May, he was arrested for attempting to close a portion of Yorkville Avenue, where it's likely he was trying to start a dance party.

In the meantime, Wendy Foikis also found herself in the spotlight; in March, she had her own feature in *The Province*. In June, she was interviewed for the *Vancouver Sun*'s weekend magazine, and later the same month, she and Foikis sat down together for a rare interview on CBC's *Take Thirty*, with host Adrienne Clarkson. She put on a brave front. But she had long since left her job at Vancouver General Hospital to be a full-time parent, leaving Foikis' grant as the couple's only source of income; and on top of that, her husband's constant travel meant she was alone with the children for months on end. Yet through it all, the media painted her support as complete and unwavering, dismissing any hint of tension in their marriage with the journalistic equivalent of a wink and a shrug, leaving her true feelings on the matter to be gleaned mostly from subtext.

"He's doing what he feels he should do," she told a *Vancouver Sun* reporter, choosing her words carefully. "It's important to him, so it means something to me. He's great with the children. But they don't get to see much of him anymore. He's so busy now."

The one time the veneer slipped for an instant was in a conversa-

tion with *Province* reporter Ann Barley. When asked if she had ever
tried to stop her husband from embarking on his fool's errand, she
snapped: "How could I? How can you stop anyone from doing what
he wants to do?"

"I will tell you right now it isn't easy," she added. "He knew where
he was going, but he didn't fully know his way."

Wendy, Martin, and Rebecca Foikis, 1968

Upon his return to Vancouver, Foikis starred in the CBC documentary short *Superfool*, by filmmaker Tom Shandel — a philosophical,
sometimes psychedelic collection of images and quotes that out-
lined his new vocation. In it, he appears taking his children to the
zoo, putting his hat on department store mannequins, clowning
around in the downtown core. Narrated by Foikis himself, it's one of
the few surviving examples of his voice to be captured on film.

"The Fool of Joy is reborn," he announced, grandly, in its opening
moments.

"Pretty indulgent film as I look at it now," Shandel later admitted,
"but aside from the rather loose structure, I meant to show Vancouver's own Eulenspiegel, the fool dressed in opposing red and blue,
carrying a mirror to reflect people back at them. [...] I took Kim's
'trip' — as we called it then — seriously. I saw basically a philosophi-

cally-inclined scholar taking it to the street. He had a big impact for sure. [...] For all the joking around, I meant to celebrate what he was doing and hoped to let him illuminate his experience on film."

Then in June, he set off for his most high-profile speaking gig yet — at the prestigious Esalen Institute in Big Sur. Esalen, the hotbed of the Human Potential Movement of the 60s, was a New Age thinkers' paradise, with a list of previous speakers that included Allen Ginsberg, Marshall McLuhan, Buckminster Fuller, and Alan Watts. Although the institute cut him a cheque for $150, Foikis only accepted $100, refusing the full amount, because in his words: "I didn't do anything." The remainder he put toward buying a ten-year-old jalopy, so he could bring his wife and children along for the ride. During the week he spent in California, he shared the Esalen grounds with Ravi Shankar and The Beatles and was asked to appear at the wedding of two Esalen staff members. And he discovered, to his surprise, how far his fame had spread; while walking the streets of Carmel, California with his family, he was stopped by Americans who had read of his exploits.

"Are you the town fool from Vancouver?" someone asked.

In July, he journeyed to Salmon Arm to judge a "paint-in" hosted by the local film society. In August, he returned to Esalen and then rounded out his summer teaching a five-week course on fairy tales at The University of British Columbia (UBC) — one encompassing two of his favourite themes, entitled "A Journey to the End of the World: Fairy Tales in Man's Eternal Quest."

"Beneath the delights of Joachim Foikis' bantering wit lies a penetrating analysis of the deeper currents which have affected man in his search for meaning and identity," the course outline read. "In this series, the town fool will focus on our rich heritage of myth and fairy tales to disclose their insights into the human condition."

By the fall, he was back at his old headquarters on the steps of the courthouse, but his rhetoric had begun to shift; now, the lifelong student was taking aim at a new target — one that would put him at odds with the educational institutions that had welcomed him throughout 1968: the education system itself.

"Education is ecstasy and ecstasy is true education," he told a reporter from the *Battle Creek Enquirer*. "But the educators that they have in the schools prevent change — that means the educators are not educators, they are hypocrites. Education is change and the educators' job in our society is to prevent change. Teachers believe madness is of the mind; madness is only of the heart."

Despite his feelings, he gave a series of talks on mythology at the Vancouver Art Gallery throughout the month of December.

"Everything is theatre in our social life except what is really important," he told a reporter. "So let's all play roles. Only in our archetypal role can we find our true identity. What I am doing in the streets is making theatre."

And sometimes, that theatre was brought directly into people's faces; in early December, Foikis crashed a public meeting of the Architectural Institute of British Columbia, attending with a huge loaf of bread and a troupe of mimes. Hosted by celebrated media personality Jack Wasserman, the event was set to feature speakers on the science of urban planning, including critic Allan Temko and UBC professor Peter Oberlander. But as Wasserman began listing each of the speakers' credentials, Foikis — in the front row with his son — shouted "Does it matter?"

Squinting, Wasserman peered into the crowd.

"Who are you?" he asked, of a young woman seated beside Foikis.

She held up a sign identifying the troupe as part of the Vancouver Living Theatre.

"I can't see from here," Wasserman replied. "What does it say?"

"I can't tell you," the girl replied. "We're supposed to be a mime troupe."

The crowd went wild.

Afterward, the troupe passed around a basket of bread, which was shared by everyone present (with the exception of Wasserman); and then, in the middle of the next presentation, Foikis announced he was leaving. This would be his final public appearance of 1968. It had been a big year, and according to *Vancouver Sun* journalist (and Greenpeace co-founder) Bob Hunter, he closed it out in style.

It was a Sunday afternoon, with Hunter and his friends — all of them parents — in one room, and their children in the other. It was a subdued affair, until Foikis arrived unannounced, with a bag full of musical instruments.

"We wanted to talk," Hunter explained. "Kids, especially small kids, can't talk the way we talk. Therefore, the invisible wall was marked with an unwritten sign that said: BEYOND THIS POINT, CHILDREN AND THEIR VIEWPOINTS ARE VERBOTEN. Before the wall could harden, however, Foikis had broken open his bag of instruments and we were all — kids and adults together — gathered in a tribal circle on the floor."

Foikis grabbed a tambourine, encouraging those gathered to choose an instrument of their own. And within minutes, the room was filled with a cacophony of wailing flutes, jingling bells, and crashing drums.

CRASH went the cymbals.

CLANG went the bells.

"None of the rest of us was a musician of any kind," Hunter admitted. "I'm tone-deaf, for one thing. And for another, like just about everybody else, I do not like to 'make a fool of myself' […] But the vortex of noise had taken shape in the middle of the room and the rest of us were drawn into it. After a while, it began to sound marvellous. None of the parts were anything to write to the Vancouver Symphony Orchestra about, but the whole thing was pure joy."

The jam went on for hours, Hunter wrote, "rippling, rising and falling, swirling, collapsing, re-forming itself. The content of the sound didn't matter at all. It became music swishing around like broken crockery, like whisk-brooms brushing the inner ear."

SWISH, they went.

BANG.

BOOM.

By the time the jam ended, it was dark, and adults and children had spent hours playing side by side. They were exhausted. But Hunter's "invisible wall" had come down.

"In large part, this is what Foikis is all about," he noted. "He goes around, causing this kind of thing to happen. If it doesn't always work, I doubt that it's his fault. People are afraid to make fools of themselves, lest the fool be recognized as being a fraction of a nerve-length too close to the real seat of the ego […] We all made fools of ourselves and became — it dawned on me later — children for one afternoon, playing with lack of purpose and only the loosest sense of time."

The year may have been finished, but Joachim Foikis certainly wasn't. 1969 was just around the corner, and he was about to make an ass of himself like never before.

3.

EPIPHANY

"The fool is a rising devil, not a fallen angel."

— Joachim Foikis, 1968

AS FAR AS CAREY LINDE CAN TELL, the inspiration for Joachim Foikis' descent into folly came to him during an acid trip. But when the pair first met in the fall of 1965 — as two of just three students in a Buddhism 400 class at UBC — Foikis seemed less like a fool and more like an intellectual.

"Kim came in dressed in professorial tweed clothes," Linde recalled. "He looked very intellectually-Germanic, I guess is the word. His stated interests were religious studies, which is why he was there. He had some degrees. He knew the Bible. He knew Blake very well. He knew Shakespeare very well. But these three intellectual paradigms occupied separate compartments in his knowledge in his brain. They wouldn't intermix — except for the odd metaphor or parable that might apply to one or the other."

Foikis readily admitted that, in his pre-fool days, he was something of an introvert — a sentiment echoed by Annie Kitaeff, who met him around the same time.

"He was just a quiet, nice guy," she noted. "Very studious. It was interesting that he chose that route because he was not an outgoing, gregarious person when we first met. He was a nice guy. Sweet, but quiet. The fact that he chose that route to make his mark was really interesting because it was completely unexpected from the person that I thought he was. Yet he drew that out of himself in order to be able to — he must have confronted himself first."

social work

BROWN, Beverly: Winnipeg,
   Manitoba
CHAPPLE, Arthur: Vancouver
DAVISON, J. M: Vancouver
DRYDEN, David L: Vancouver

FOJKIS, Joachim: Vancouver
GHAN, Sherman L: Weyburn,
   Saskatchewan
GRIFFITHS, Lois J: Rocky Ford, Alberta
HANOWSKI, A. J: Vancouver

Joachim Foikis, 1962. Image Courtesy of *The Totem*.

Luckily, for students looking to confront themselves, there were few places better than the Buddhism 400 class of Arthur Link. A professor of religious studies, Link was an American expat and expert on Buddhist thought who had translated several key texts on the subject and had recently left the University of Michigan for a safe haven in Canada, after his affinity for Eastern traditions had led to rumours that he was a communist. With his bald pate, Link looked like he belonged to an older generation, but his eyes betrayed a glint of boyish mischief, and from their first class together, Linde sensed a kindred spirit.

"The very first one hour that we had with Arthur, we got into a discussion about LSD," he said. "Right off the bat — we didn't bring it up. We just talked about Buddhism in modern day and how do you experience transcendence — meditative things. We were talking about it from day one."

Linde had already been experimenting with psychedelic drugs himself, having taken a year off to hunt magic mushrooms in Mexico, before discovering to his surprise that they grew in abundance right on the UBC grounds. And LSD, legal in Canada until 1968, was already gaining popularity — particularly amongst middle-class (mostly white) university students. Many of its early proponents were academics of some kind — Timothy Leary was a clinical psychologist at Harvard, and the Merry Pranksters' Ken Kesey had first tried it during an experiment while still a student at Stanford. The Acid Tests, later immortalized in Tom Wolfe's book, were already proceeding in earnest by the time Foikis and Linde sat down in the fall of 1965. And by 1966, a survey conducted by the Narcotic Addiction Foundation found that LSD use amongst university students had increased dramatically — including at least 100 people at UBC. The proliferation of psychedelic drugs within West Coast counterculture was just one indication of the seismic cultural shift that was taking place across the country — one that was playing out on a smaller scale within the city itself. In the mayor's chair sat Tom Campbell, an aggressive, cantankerous blowhard who found himself constantly at war in the news (and sometimes in person) with the city's youth and counterculture. Like many of Vancouver's mayors, Campbell was a property developer, and with his slicked-back hair and ready sneer, he epitomized the values of an older generation. These same values filled the pages of the two major dailies — the *Vancouver Sun* and *The Province* — whose columnists, stodgy in their suits and glasses, regularly ran stories bemoaning the decline of the city's youth.

Meanwhile, the houses along Fourth Avenue in Kitsilano had become home to the burgeoning hippie movement. Known colloquially as "Acid Row," the stretch between Arbutus and Yew Streets grew into something of a tourist attraction — home to more than a thousand hippies by some estimates — as gawkers would cruise the neighbourhood hoping to catch a glimpse of the counterculture. Vancouver's hippie scene was a virtual carbon copy of the one in San Francisco's Haight-Ashbury neighbourhood and tended to espouse the same values: free love, a disdain for money and private property, an appetite for protest, a predilection for psychedelic drugs, and the use of their own bodies as a social and political statement (some hippies grew their hair to such extremes that a Vancouver barber briefly offered free haircuts; the offer had no takers). The music scene too followed the Haight-Ashbury example, birthing local bands like Papa Bear's Medicine Show, Mother Tucker's Yellow Duck, and The Seeds of Time. When asked about Kitsilano's hippie population, Tom Campbell — as usual — didn't mince words.

"I think society is entitled to use everything that is available to it in order to stamp out this cancerous growth that is invading society," he grumbled.

As the movement grew, it nurtured its own set of advocates: like *The Georgia Straight* correspondent Korky Day, who helped spearhead the effort to turn Wreck Beach into a nudist enclave, and student activist Stan Persky, who was a regular thorn in the side of city magistrates and administrators. And despite Tom Campbell's dim view, it also swept up a number of university intellectuals — not just students, but professors, like UBC philosopher Arthur Link. Into the late 60s, Kitsilano would remain ground zero for the hippie movement, served by businesses like the Psychedelic Shop, restaurant mainstays like The Naam, and the Cool-Aid house on Fourth, which provided free lodging and medical care to transient youth.

But tensions continued to mount. In the face of the hippie invasion, the Vancouver School Board launched an intensive drug education program, speaking in alarmist tones about drugs like LSD.

In an open letter to the newspapers, city medical health officer Dr. J.L. Gayton made a series of apocalyptic pronouncements. City council even convened a special "hippie committee" to examine the issue.

"We suffered through a summer of heartbreak and horror as the element swarmed in to create a nuisance," cried Kitsilano Ratepayers' Association president Harold Kidd, in an interview with *The Province*, "disregarding the law and order; living more like animals than humans; disregarding and disrupting businesses; bringing LSD, marijuana, heroin, and other illegal drugs in our community."

But the relationship between science, academia, and psychedelics in Western Canada was a closer one than in most other places; as far back as the 1940s, New Westminster's Hollywood Hospital had been performing psychiatric interventions using LSD, achieving remarkable results in everything from spousal abuse to alcoholism. Therefore, against that backdrop, perhaps what happened next wasn't particularly surprising.

"Then in the spring," Carey Linde noted, "we agreed that we would all go to Arthur's house and have our final exam by dropping a mega dose of LSD."

So, in the spring of 1966, Joachim Foikis joined Link, Linde, and fellow student Erik Kalaidzis at Link's home, to begin his final exam. It would be the last he ever took, and it heralded the end of his academic career.

"Arthur's house was an incredible place for psychedelics," Linde later said. "He had brought back from China these beautiful pieces. I never forget the carpet in his living room was a big blue rug with Chinese designs. You couldn't have designed a better place to do it."

After some preparation, all four of them lay down on Link's living room rug and held hands. According to Linde's recollection, they each took 800 mcg — eight times the amount normally used during an acid trip — a dose designed to induce a phenomenon akin to nirvana known as ego death.

"We lay down on the floor in a cross, on our backs with our heads in the center, touching," he said. "All four of our heads were touching, and we were holding hands with the person next to us. We had some small pillows. We spent — I couldn't tell you — two, three, four hours like that. We all went through our own individual experiences. There were periods in there when, looking back at it, we think we shared experiences."

But the journey wasn't always a pleasant one.

"At one point, Kim was going through some troubling moments," Linde recalled. "I remember asking him how it was all going. I know he said he was up on the cross. He was up to be crucified. I can't recall whether he said he went through the crucifixion — because that's recognized as a key moment in drugs and Buddhist meditation. When the ego dies, if the ego was protecting you, it saves itself, as in: 'you're not going to kill me that easily.' It's conceivable that somehow that's what happened. He experienced it as having a nail driven through him."

It's difficult not to place this moment within the context of his recent tragedy; it had been just two years since Foikis had put Karen in the ground, and suddenly he was being inundated with images of guilt, suffering, sacrifice. A cosmic conspiracy.

As the trip entered its fourth hour, Link, Linde, and Kalaidzis managed to get to their feet and move to the kitchen. Foikis, however, stayed behind, lost in his own thoughts.

"And as he was lying there, every once in a while, he'd giggle," Linde mused, "and he'd say, 'Ooop! There goes Blake.' Then there'd be a long time period and he'd say, 'There goes Shakespeare!'"

Eventually, Foikis joined his peers, and they sat down around the kitchen table, discussing their experiences in detail. Some had been shared, others individual.

"At some point, we came around to Kim," Linde later explained, "and he said that he realized he'd just thrown these things away when he was saying, 'There goes Blake.' He just chucked all his knowledge out."

When asked why, Foikis replied: "It's useless. It was of no value whatsoever." Then, he chuckled to himself and said: "I feel like a fool."

"When he said: 'I feel like a fool,' I recall it as being almost immediate," Linde recalled. "That he tossed off all that he had been entrusted with by university courses, by subjects, certain pigeon-holes, that whole approach; a degree in this, a degree in that — everything melded into one in his head. What came out was an amalgam of the best of religion — whether it was the Bible, Judaism, or Buddhism. Whether it was Blake, who was profound, or Shake-speare. They all were mixed up into one great soup, out of which sprang, in red and blue and bells, the fool — formerly Kim Foikis."

In Linde's mind, the experience was a transformative one, an epiphany, a moment of delineation between the old Kim Foikis and the new. But if Foikis himself ever saw it that way, he never admitted as much.

"I took [acid] a year ago," he told a reporter in 1967, "but it only verified my natural mysticism."

As his fame grew, he was inevitably confronted with questions about his drug use, but he maintained that his state of mind came from somewhere else. "I get high on Mother Goose, not drugs," he once told a reporter. "Religion should not be the opium of the people, but neither should opium be the religion of the people."

In any case, he seemed to have put the trip behind him — at least briefly — taking the summer off before returning once more to UBC — this time for a one-year postgraduate degree in library sciences, alongside Annie Kitaeff. He stayed far away from the world of the Fourth Avenue hippies, as they packed onto the PNE Grounds and danced to the Grateful Dead and Janis Joplin. As late as January 1967, he was still firmly on that path, authoring articles for a library sciences magazine, just a few months away from a good job with a decent salary. For now, Blake was gone. Shakespeare was gone. Like the rest of the world, Vancouver was a place awash with folly, a city where the dark fool lurked around every corner.

But not for long.

For Joachim Foikis, the cock had crowed.

'Twas time to rise.

"Kim Foikis Is a Man Who Radiates Life"

**— an excerpt from *The Globe and Mail*,
by Nancy Beckett, September 12, 1967.**

Joachim Foikis, 1967

Kim Foikis is a man who radiates life; who is life. You can only
sense this in talking with him and observing him; you can't pin it

down to specific words or actions. He is in himself a tremendous life-force. He represents what I could call the new life: the sort of upsurge or renaissance, that is the goal (rarely achieved) of the hippies. Life seen through his eyes is heightened, creative, multi-colored.

Kim is basically a theologian, a man of God: his concern, in a very real sense, is to save men's souls. Men today are dead, not because they have sinned and cut themselves off from God — there is hope for the sinners, for at least they feel that God exists — but because they have fallen asleep. They have lost touch with life. The majority of Canadians are slaves to a shallow and dehumanizing set of values, and to the fear of giving or risking anything.

To these people Kim is a threat; because he represents what man could be. They recognize his superiority by hating him or laughing at him; he is dangerous because he is alive. He bothers their conscience. His very existence, his bold presence in a bright red-and-blue costume, is for dead people a judgement — seeing him, they are forced to judge themselves.

Those who are alive, or at least trying to be, recognize in Kim a sort of spiritual leader. Children, of course, flock to him, drawn to the magnetism that any truly great man has for children. The hippies, who are trying to preserve or recapture a childlike innocence within an adult's rational frame of reference, seem to have much the same instinctive trust in him. And all those people, young or old, who are dissatisfied with the material, success-oriented values of our society and seek something better, willingly recognize Kim's true worth.

Certainly, it is impossible not to react to this man. Either he is a threat to your whole concept of life and your system of values, or he is absolutely right. I think he is right. I think that such a man knows the secret of eternal life — the state of being in total harmony with life itself, with energy, creativity, creation. People such as he who actually come somewhere close to living it will be from such people that new life will grow in this world.

A FOOL AND HIS MONEY

"It is foolishness that man should be the servant of money. Money should be the servant of man."

— Joachim Foikis,
The Vancouver Sun Weekend Magazine, 1968

12.

GREAT FALL (Part Two)

"His eyes do show his days are almost done."

—Feste, *Twelfth Night*

IT WAS A SUNNY DAY IN MAY 2007, and Joachim Foikis was about to turn himself upside down.

The blue of the waves below glistened, and the bustle of tourists made Victoria's Inner Harbour — a place surrounded by century-old buildings that dripped with righteous self-importance — feel more like a carnival sideshow.

He was seventy-two years old. Tall. Soft-spoken, with an unmistakable German accent. His face, never one that had taken easily to smiling, now somehow seemed even more serious, his once-sharp features weathered by years of poverty. And his eyes, peering out from a pair of thick, round-framed glasses, had taken on a somewhat mournful look. Just moments earlier, he had been a self-described "bookworm" living a quiet life in a communal house in nearby Esquimalt. An avid gardener. A pensioner with few remaining family connections, wearing donated clothes and making art from scavenged items like driftwood and bottlecaps.

Then, he saw the band.

Their drums banged and their cymbals crashed.

Strolling along the Inner Harbour with friends — including long-time friend Gary Hano — he heard music. And he began to dance.

CRASH went the cymbals.

BOOM went the drums.

A foolish choice, perhaps, at his age; the roads and boardwalk of the Inner Harbour are built well above the water — in most places, as much as two storeys — to give tourists a panoramic view of the horizon. Only a month earlier, while goofing around with friends, a seventeen-year-old high school student had fallen from the same spot and ended up in critical condition at Victoria General Hospital. The exact sequence of events is unknown; the only account of what happened comes from Hano, who spoke briefly about the incident to *The Globe and Mail* journalist Rod Mickleburgh. What's known for certain is that he died dancing. Losing his footing, Foikis stumbled and fell two storeys onto the rocks below. While details are scant, it's easy to imagine those last few seconds: his eyes taking on that familiar glint of mischief, of life — radiating. Of each movement throwing off the weight of years. He stood on a wall. Then, a slip. A stumble.

CRASH. BANG. BOOM.

And a great fall.

There was no obituary. The incident never made the Victoria papers. The only mention of it was more than a month later, as part of Mickleburgh's article in *The Globe and Mail*.

"There was a band down there, and he was dancing," Hanno said, simply. "He took a tumble."

Upon hearing the details of his passing, longtime friend Carey Linde felt a twinge of guilt.

"I regret that I didn't spend more time with him," he sighed. "I knew at some point that he had moved to Victoria, and I heard later he'd died there. But we'd lost touch."

"Well, that's the way he would have wanted to go," former neighbour Cindy Taylor said, upon hearing the news. "Funny 'til the last."

He died dancing. Foolish, perhaps. But Joachim Foikis had always been a fool. It had cost him his marriage, his children, his public profile — and in the eyes of some — his sanity. It had left him homeless and landed him in court more than once. Although his legacy had been largely forgotten in the forty years since his fateful vision, he had, in a small way, for a short time, turned the city — and the world — upside down, with a song in his heart and a drum in his hand.

But all of that had come and gone.

Now, he was dancing. Dancing toward the end.

He was stumbling. He was falling. He was upside down in this world.

And all the king's horses and all the king's men couldn't put Joachim Foikis together again.

7.

PETER AND PAN

"May not an ass know when the cart draws the horse?"

—The Fool, *King Lear*

IT BEGAN WITH A CRUNCH.

It was mid-April 1969, and Joachim Foikis was in Burnaby — on his way home from a lecture at Simon Fraser University entitled "The Fool Has the Last Word" — when he collided with a female driver at the corner of Gilmore and Parker Streets. Luckily, no one was injured, but the front end of Foikis' car — the ten-year-old jalopy he had purchased for his trip to Esalen — was destroyed. And rather than spend what little remained of his grant on a new car, he decided to take things in a different direction; at the scene, he noted, it was time to "give up the car for a slower, but safer, donkey."

"He has been seeking one for some time," Wendy told *The Province*. "An old one with a quiet disposition."

This wasn't without precedent in the fool tradition; Turkish phil-

osopher Mulla Nasrudin used donkeys as his main mode of convey-
ance during the thirteenth century. Statues of him often show him
astride a donkey, and they appear in many of the stories and anecdotes in his canon.

At first, Foikis had his eye on a single donkey from the Fraser Valley — even requesting that the City provide a home for it in Stanley
Park — but less than two weeks later, he had changed his tune, buying a pair of them (along with two sets of harnesses and a cart) for
$250 from Salt Spring Island resident Werner Luth. They were
young, impetuous, stubborn. He renamed them "Peter" and "Pan,"
and his first act was to ride them from the ferry terminal right up to
the steps of City Hall.

Joachim Foikis, with Peter and Pan, 1969.
Image Courtesy of Postmedia, *Vancouver Sun Archives*

"Downtown rush-hour motorists Friday were the first to experience
coexistence between horse-powered engines and donkey-powered carts
when Foikis went out for a test drive," the *Vancouver Sun* reported.

"They rested — sometimes after only a few hoof-clops — in bus zones, intersections, and in any lane they happened to be travelling."

"Little work was done at City Hall Friday afternoon after town fool Joachim Foikis arrived there with his newly-purchased donkeys, Peter and Pan," added *The Province*. "Employees lined the windows of City Hall, and passing motorists did a double take as they saw Foikis and the donkeys near the City Hall steps."

"Take them up into the council chambers," remarked a middle-aged man, walking past the scene. "They wouldn't know the difference."

For his part, Foikis was jubilant, vowing to spend the summer travelling the city in his "gypsy caravan."

"I've solved both my housing and transportation problems," he grinned, in an interview with *The Province*.

Even the irascible Tom Campbell seemed amused, remarking: "If the fool wants to live with mules, it's up to him. It seems like birds of a feather."

Despite Campbell's seemingly laissez-faire attitude, municipal ordnance frowned on the keeping of livestock in the city; and from the moment Peter and Pan arrived, they became an easy target for magistrates and bylaw officers.

"Donkeys aren't supposed to be running loose in the city," a police officer told him on one occasion.

Foikis cocked his head. "Do you mean to say there are no asses running around this city?"

On another occasion, he was stopped by a magistrate and issued a ticket after Peter and Pan left a sizeable collection of droppings on the sidewalk.

"Sir, your donkeys are polluting my city," the magistrate grimaced.

"Sir," Foikis replied, "your city is polluting my donkeys."

"They were saying: 'Well, you can't have these in the city,'" Carey Linde recalled. "He had to move them sometimes from place to place through the alleys and hide them in people's backyards. Various people kept these things in their backyard, but everybody in the neighbour-hood was in full support, so nobody ratted on him. It was amazing."

Through the spring, Foikis was as good as his word, using his donkeys to trim people's lawns and giving rides to anyone who asked — sometimes adults (often drunken revellers in Gastown), but most often children.

"The donkeys are a delight to children," he told reporters. "They lead them around and sometimes parents give their children a ride on them."

But the donkeys were also unpredictable and prone to dramatic escape attempts; they escaped from his yard in mid-May, and a week or so later (when Foikis left them in the care of his friend and neigh-bour Mary Summerville) they slipped their tethers and took off at a gallop down Thirteenth Avenue — sparking a chase that went on for seven blocks before Summerville and several other neighbours man-aged to get them back.

"I've got this big lawn full of grass, and I thought we'd do each other a favour," she told reporters. "But a neighbour and I decided to change their ropes and they took off on us. I caught the small one — Peter — and grabbed his rope. Boy, is he stubborn. I was really going — at least six-foot strides."

She chuckled.

"Now I know how it feels to be the town fool. It was quite a job to get back home."

A few weeks later, they escaped again; this time from the yard of an elderly friend, CBC technician Ib Birkefeldt, who had requested them to help trim his lawn. But by now, the law was watching; seeing the donkeys wandering down Seventh Avenue, a neighbour phoned in a complaint, and they were taken to the city pound. When he heard the news, Foikis was furious.

"An elderly gentleman there asked me to bring my two donkeys over to cut down the grass in front of his large lot as the city apparently wouldn't do it," he fumed. "It was a dirty trick by the city to take my donkeys away."

Nonetheless, he used what little remained of his grant to bail them out. Despite his attempts to move them around — first to Saturna Island, then the Interior — they were impounded on three subsequent occasions between June and August.

"If they're going to be kept here, they'll have to be looked after twenty-four hours a day," a police officer warned him.

"I can't sleep with them," Foikis protested.

"Then you had better sleep pretty close to them."

On August 14, they were impounded for the final time after being picked up by the corner of Second Avenue and Stephens Street, near Kitsilano Beach. But by this point, Foikis could no longer bail them out. He was broke, the last of his grant money long since spent on a single, grandiose gesture — a dance party to end all dance parties. After more than a week in impound, Peter and Pan were sent to auction. Alongside thirty-five other bidders — a collection of farmers and curious hippies — Joachim Foikis arrived to watch the proceedings "with a tear in his eye."

The opening bid was for two carrots.

"These aren't just ordinary asses," joked auctioneer George Masse. "These are famous asses."

Despite a brief bidding war, Peter and Pan were sold to an unidentified "mystery man" in a white shirt for $120. When questioned by a reporter from *The Province*, the man said little — only that he was taking them back to Salt Spring Island.

It's "the end of a happening," Foikis said. "They did good service during the summer. They now need a good winter pasture. They turned on a lot of people who never saw an ass before. I got them for the children."

In the end, it wasn't a complete loss; Foikis took home the bulk of the sale price — $101.

And even though he was out of money, and quickly running out of time, Foikis was confident that this "happening" wouldn't be his last.

"Next year," he smiled, "maybe I'll get an elephant."

10.

MAGIC MOUNTAIN

"For fools a mirror shall it be,
Where each his counterfeit may see.
The glass of fools the truth may show."

— Sebastian Brant, *Ship of Fools*

IT WAS 1970, and thirty-eight-year-old Joachim Foikis had just arrived in Toronto, looking to start over.

His fool days had just come to an abrupt end; while on a plane to Europe, en route to visit his now-estranged family, he "felt it leave him."

"He said all of a sudden, he just felt it go," longtime friend Laurence Fisher explained. "He didn't really know it was there — he just felt it when it went. He said he doesn't know what it was — maybe he smoked too much hash or something — but he said that while he was being the fool, he was touched. He told me that his full realization of that — he was in that place — only came when he fell out of it. And when it stopped, he noticed."

Later in life, Foikis had a simpler assessment, telling journalist Kathy Tait: "I didn't want to become a cliché of myself."

He had no firm plans upon his arrival, and between 1970 and 1975, he hitchhiked across the country more than once. He spent time squatting in a cabin on Bowen Island with a group of hippies (quite possibly the "company of fools" he'd been spotted with near the end of 1969) until the landlord burned it down. He briefly lived with a woman and her three children and made several trips back and forth between Lasqueti Island and Toronto's notorious Rochdale College.

Rochdale in the early 1970s was a place that would have seemed tailor-made for someone like Foikis. Standing at the corner of Bloor and Huron Streets, it was originally intended to solve the University of Toronto's student housing problem, but instead became a bizarre experiment in peer-led education and co-op living.

"The philosophy of freedom and collective responsibility will form the backbone of Rochdale College," representatives told the *Toronto Star*. "Students will live and study without the usual formalities of classes and grades."

Overseen by Campus Co-op, a self-funded, student-led housing provider, Rochdale was initially turned into an educational facility in order to circumvent $175,000 in property taxes. Its founders built an informal, ad-hoc system that revolved around communal housing, student "resource people," and "non-degrees" in a variety of subjects that could be purchased for next to nothing. Unsurprisingly, when it opened its doors in 1968, Rochdale attracted a number of fringe figures (by one estimate, twenty per cent of its residents were American draft dodgers) and a significant amount of squatters. Rent was low, tuition was nonexistent, and the building featured amenities like community gardens, a daycare, a ceramics studio, and clothing-optional rooftop sunbathing. The bottom two floors were reserved for social activities, and each floor was divided into units of a dozen ashrams (AKA bedrooms), responsible for their own rent collection and cleanup. By the time Foikis arrived in 1970, the building had become a haven for Toronto's creatives and counterculture figures — and had become remarkably self-contained, by then even having its own free clinic.

"I've talked to people who would go weeks at a time, months even, without going outside, because everything was in the building," pop-culture historian Stuart Henderson later explained. "And we're talking from childcare all the way to maternity doctors. People would give birth at Rochdale."

For the seven years it operated, Rochdale's doors remained open to anyone and everyone — which meant that, in addition to squatters like Foikis, it soon became a haven for drug dealers. By 1971, Rochdale had evolved into what the CBC called: "North America's largest drug distribution warehouse. Hash, pot, and LSD are in large supply. The Rochdale security force includes members of biker gangs."

Crime continued to flourish; there were stories of overdoses and police raids. There were at least six suicides, and in December 1971, a twenty-three-year-old former model and mother named Marika Sokoloski was stabbed to death. There are few indications of Foikis' activities during this time, other than his tending a garden plot with several other Rochdale residents. Then, in 1975, Rochdale defaulted on its mortgage. In May, police showed up with sledgehammers, breaking down doors and serving the sixty remaining residents with eviction notices.

"Evicted tenants milled in front of the building shouting obscenities," reported the *Toronto Star*. "Many women carried babies and were surrounded by their possessions, including many cats and dogs."

"People never knew about the education side of Rochdale because the papers didn't find that dramatic or sensational enough to print," protested resident Jim Washington, who had travelled from Chicago to study at the institution. "But the creativity really came together there. It was a good atmosphere. […] I got a Rochdale degree in revolutionary engineering. It is the only degree I care to have."

By then, Joachim Foikis was elsewhere — likely in England visiting his family, for what would turn out to be the final time. A 1972 article in the *Toronto Star* had erroneously reported that he and Wendy were still together and that she "completely support[ed] his courage and dedication." But the truth was, Foikis hadn't seen his family in years. The visit in 1975 would be his final, and after this, neither Wendy nor Rebecca would make any effort to speak to him ever again.

In the meantime, Vancouver's counterculture kept pushing for a fool; in 1974, the Peanut Party ran a joke candidate named "Mr. Peanut," who sang and danced at rallies alongside Myrna Peanut and The Peanettes. Gastown fixture "Gentleman Jim" Land urged voters to mark a black X on the back of their ballots to indicate their willingness to nominate him for town fool. The following year, a group calling themselves the Earthling Survival Party took up the charge, declaring that "The city will have to acknowledge that there is a desire for Vancouver to have an official fool."

But Foikis was nowhere to be found. His decision to abandon the city puzzled many — journalists and friends alike. One even went so far as to label it "self-imposed exile." Rumours swirled that he inhabited a shack with "Lyn, the sweetest of nymphets." On more than one occasion, longtime friend Carey Linde would call it madness. So what had brought about his retreat from society? Was it drugs? The tragic loss of his family? Insanity? Or was it something deeper? Was he still haunted by memories of Karen, a ghostly image from his past, long since vanished?

Whatever the reason, it's likely that Foikis landed on Lasqueti Island sometime in 1975. He had visited before, during his time criss-crossing the country, and Lasqueti — like Rochdale — would have been a perfect place for him to settle in. Briefly a resource community, it was all but abandoned by the 1970s, when it began to attract others like Foikis, who were hoping to escape the day-to-day monotony of city living. At the time, it was home to fewer than one hundred people, a heavily-logged landscape of feral sheep and absentee landowners. There was no power grid. No water. No sewage. No infrastructure of any kind, apart from a marina, a church, and a school. The nearest doctor's office was on Vancouver Island, a one-hour ferry ride away. But for the collection of artists, eccentrics, and freethinkers who flocked to its shores in the early 1970s looking to get back to the land, it was a new Garden of Eden. Other such communities were springing up across BC, trying to expand on the ideals of the 1960s; places with names like Cosmic Debris, Rainbow Family, and Chicken Crest. When he arrived, Foikis would have been in good company, meeting neighbours with names like Zootie, "Boho Ron" Lawton, Brother Richard, and Countess Kolbassa. The new arrivals were frank about bodily functions and comfortable with nudity, drug use, and sexual experimentation. Some drank their own urine, claiming it had medicinal properties. And amongst them, noted early settler Doug Hamilton, there was a "tolerance for extreme personalities, odd characters, and strongly held beliefs." It was even briefly home to a cult — profiled in a 1970 issue of *Maclean's* — made up of disenchanted young professionals (most of them women), presided over by a man named Ted Sideras.

Most of Lasqueti's new arrivals had never embarked on such an ambitious experiment before, possessing few survival skills, and in the early years, the learning curve was steep. Basic concepts like sanitation and construction had to be learned the hard way. Some grew marijuana — occasionally attracting the attention of a passing police helicopter. Between 1970 and 1975, the community grew at a rapid rate, coalescing into a series of distinct regions, amongst them The Mudflats, The South End, and — most crucially for Foikis — Fisher-land. Prior to the hippie invasion, the property had been in Laurence Fisher's family for generations; in the mid-1890s, after a voyage across the Pacific, his grandfather had sailed past Lasqueti Island and immediately liked what he saw.

"He said, 'I like the look of that,'" Fisher explained. "The skipper put him out on his canoe and said, 'Pick him up in a week.' Grandpa rowed over to Lasqueti, and there was a guy sitting and smoking his pipe on the beach. My grandfather said, 'A lovely place you have here,' and the guy said, 'Yes. You want to buy it?'"

Fisher himself had inherited the property at thirteen, following the early death of his father and a great uncle who held the title. He'd made the occasional visit, but in 1971, following his graduation from university, he moved to the island full-time with his wife Kathy, his mother Judith, and their children.

"It was a really small community in those days," he said. "It was only basically in the early 70s that things picked up, and by '71 it was getting to be — probably there was a few dozen hippies. Maybe more. By '72, there was about seventy hippies that had moved up, and there was about seventy old-timers still living here."

But for an idealist like Fisher, it wasn't enough to make a home on Lasqueti; he wanted to build a community.

"I walked around [the property] when I moved back here," he recalled. "I could walk around it all day and not cross the lines. It was really disturbing. If I had inherited ten acres, I could stick a fence around it, and I'd be happy as a clown. You walk around the land that you can't cross the boundary of, that's kind of a lie. You have to do something about it."

What Fisher did is turn the land into a co-op. It started small, with only seventeen members, but over time it grew, eventually including a sawmill, a woodworking shop, and a number of other members. At first it was known simply as the Land Company, but in time, it was rechristened "Magic Mountain."

"It was very rudimentary, really," Fisher admits. "There was half a dozen or so couples who were starting to build a house here at that time. That was the beginning of the co-op."

And it was around this time, Fisher recalls, that Joachim Foikis decided to settle down. He arrived alongside a friend named Tim Montella. Montella and Foikis had met during his time at Rochdale, and after the college collapsed, Foikis convinced his friend — suffering from schizophrenia — to join him in the small, laid-back community emerging on the island.

"Kim brought him here," Fisher said, "because he thought it'd be a good place for him to be."

While Foikis wasn't a member of the co-op, Fisher gave him permission to occupy a small cabin in nearby Scotty Bay for just $300 per year. His cabin was even more rudimentary than most, and, like the others, lacked electricity and running water. But Foikis seems to have thrived; while many of the early back-to-the-land proponents later returned to the city, Foikis spent the next eight years in his cabin on Scotty Bay, tending his two garden plots and selling the overflow at farmer's markets on Vancouver Island. And it was in one of those Scotty Bay garden plots that he met Cindy Taylor. Taylor was in her late twenties when she arrived on Lasqueti in 1983, moving into a small cabin up the road — just a five-minute walk from her new neighbour. They developed a strong friendship over the next six years; Foikis gifted Taylor a portion of his garden plot, and on Tuesday nights, he babysat her two children while Taylor and her partner played volleyball.

"He taught me how to garden," she recalled, "and he was a good teacher. I still use a lot of the things that he told me. He knew what he was doing, and we also had limited water source. He taught me how to conserve water and many aspects of gardening that you might not learn in the city. He knew all about it. It was all organic. He knew about the pests, he knew about watering, he knew about fertilizing. He'd go across to Parksville, and he'd get whatever he needed for gardening and bring it back."

At the time, Foikis was still selling produce on Vancouver Island. But as Taylor recalled, he may also have gotten over his aversion to taking welfare payments.

"He had money," she noted. "He could take the ferry over to Vancouver Island every couple of weeks and do his laundry and get groceries and things like that. He had to pay the Land Company three hundred bucks a year or something. He did have to work over some bills at certain points in a year. I don't know if he had managed to get some disability pension maybe, somehow. He was good at working the system. He knew what he could get."

And in spite of the narrative in the Vancouver papers, Foikis wasn't wasting away in self-imposed exile. He was flourishing. He socialized with his neighbours. His clothes were clean and well cared for. He took part in dances at the community hall. He enjoyed a few pints here and there.

"He was really well-liked, and everybody knew him," Taylor said. "He loved to socialize and talk. He had his political interest always. He appreciated intelligent conversation and he did keep to himself, but he went around often enough that he wasn't a recluse or anything. We never had to go looking for him. He was always around. We'd see him every day. The garden was right there, so he'd be down in his garden every day. We'd see him there, and I don't think many days went by that we didn't see him."

According to Taylor, Foikis left Lasqueti in approximately 1989, heading back to Vancouver after an absence of twenty years. In the wake of his departure, Lasqueti remained as independent as ever. Tim Montella stayed behind, living on the island until his death in

2018. The Magic Mountain Land Co-op continued to evolve, eventually becoming home to a free store, a recycling depot, and a nursing station. In 2018, many of its aging members began preparing for the end, creating Good to Go kits to help their loved ones deal with their affairs and remains.

Foikis and Cindy Taylor kept in touch into the 1990s, until Taylor herself left Lasqueti Island to settle in the Okanagan. And, when asked to recount stories of her friend and neighbour, she couldn't help but chuckle to herself.

"His favourite story was the time that he took a donkey into the courthouse," she laughed. "He went in and the judge said, 'get that donkey out of the courthouse. Your donkey is polluting my courthouse.' Kim says, 'Your courthouse is polluting my donkey.' The judge, he said, 'What are you doing in here with that ridiculous outfit? Get out of here.' Kim says, 'My ridiculous outfit? What about your ridiculous outfit?'"

She laughed again. "He used to say: 'In the halls of justice, the justice is in the halls.' That was one of his favourite sayings."

$4.$

VALENTINE'S DAY

"Motley's the only wear."

— Touchstone, *As You Like It*

IT WAS VALENTINE'S DAY, and Joachim Foikis had just seen something that would turn his world upside down.

It came to him in the middle of the day, during a stroll with Wendy and the children, what he later called "a fantastic vision where everything was turned outside in."

"I had an epiphany on the fourteenth of February last year," he told *The New York Times*. "I saw an archetypal vision of the fool. I was high for six weeks."

During later interviews, he would provide contradictory accounts of that fateful vision — sometimes he'd claim to have seen an archetypal fool, other times, an angel. But in any event, the experience set him down a new path.

"Suddenly," he said, "it came to me. I saw that I had to invert the existing social order and reverse its values."

As his fame grew, he would often speak of his desire to create a character, a modern legend heavily informed by his study of theology and literature — equal parts philosopher and merry prankster. And he knew exactly where to start.

"Joachim announced his decision 'Just like that,'" an article in *The Province* reported. "He was going to become the town fool, and without more ado, they roared off to town to buy some material for his costume."

And in the days that followed, his wife Wendy dutifully sewed him two outfits — one to wear and one to wash — painted, at Foikis' insistence, half red and half blue.

"I call it 'joyful symmetry,'" he said at the time. "The red symbolizes the blood and the flesh. And the blue symbolizes vision, spirit. Thus, the integration of body and spirit. The marriage of heaven and hell [...] My costume is my medium. I put this costume on my back to add a little bit of red-and-blue — to add a little bit of colour to this city."

And while the newspapers presented the choice as sudden, decisive, and clear-cut, it would be some time before Wendy Foikis grasped the full scope of her husband's plan.

"She thought I was going to be in a play at UBC," he admitted, years later. "She didn't know I was going to put this thing on and walk down the street."

She would soon find out; with just six weeks to go before graduation, Foikis quit university. Each morning, he would don his fool's motley and ride the bus from their cozy cottage on Fifteenth Avenue to the steps of the downtown courthouse, where he would spend the afternoon conversing about meaning and folly with anyone who cared to engage. But for a soft-spoken academic like Foikis, it wasn't the most natural of transitions.

"I'd always been an introverted bookworm until then," he said, of his first weeks on the job. "It took a lot of guts to appear publicly like this."

"What I remember about his manner was that he didn't come across as someone who laughed a lot," mused Rick Kitaeff, Annie's husband, and one of the founders of hippie newspaper *The Georgia Straight*. "His appearance was actually kind of severe."

But for many who encountered him, it was precisely this gentle, thoughtful nature that made him captivating.

"To be the fool, he had to confront people," said Annie Kitaeff. "He had to be not aggressive, but he had to take the initiative with people and wear the fool's costume, which made him very visible, to say the least, and to make himself the centre of attention in that way. That was just an unexpected avenue for him to take. I would have expected somebody who was far more gregarious and outgoing would do what he did, would make the choices he did. In retrospect, it was actually somebody who was gregarious and outgoing wouldn't really be as likely to do that. It's somebody who is interior, who is philosophical, who is studious, and who does confront himself with the essential nature of life who would become the fool."

He quickly settled into a routine: 2:00 p.m. to 3:00 p.m. on the courthouse steps ("The fool and the law agree very well together," he often said), with the rest of the afternoon spent wandering the streets, bauble in hand — a gift from a Gastown cobbler — fulfilling his new mission of spreading joy and confusion. During the spring and summer of 1967, the area surrounding the courthouse fountain had become a gathering place for transient youth — low-income men and women, as well as a healthy smattering of hippies — bemoaned by the local papers and Tom Campbell, and occasionally the site of clashes between young people and the police. But Joachim Foikis, with his cap and bells, existed in a space outside of both the establishment and the counterculture. And in the beginning, the attention he attracted wasn't always positive.

"At first the hippies all thought I was a police informer," he chuckled. "The rest of the city saw me as a crackpot."

"He was from an older generation, which put him at odds with the hippies, in a way," Rick Kitaeff later said. "They had that idea that anyone over thirty you can't trust."

"Hippies were conformists in their own way," Annie added. "Also, they were very fuzzy sometimes in their thinking. Oh, 'Love everybody. Turn on, turn in. Just hang out, chill,' but Kim was insisting on clarity. Focus on the moment, focus on the truth within yourself. Even in those weird times, that was very weird."

All the same, when Annie Kitaeff first encountered her old classmate on the courthouse steps, she found the experience profoundly unsettling.

"Yeah, at the time, it made me uncomfortable," she admitted. "Actually, that was one of the goals, I think, to make people uncomfortable; because if you're uncomfortable, you'll start questioning, and if you're not — if you're very comfortable — you're not going to bother questioning him. Now looking back, I see what he was doing, and, in a way, it was really brilliant."

Courthouse Fountain, 1967. Image Courtesy of the Vancouver Archives

For his part, Foikis didn't think too highly of the hippies either.

"The negative aspect of the hippies is that there are those who have dropped out of society because they are too lazy to work," he said, "not because they are restless and trying to change things. You can only transform society if you work at it."

Indeed, he would often refer to himself as "a drop in rather than a drop out from society," noting: "I prefer to think of myself as I have dropped into the life of the city."

But it wasn't just Annie Kitaeff and the hippies of the courthouse square who were uncomfortable with Foikis' behaviour. Shortly after her husband took to the streets, Wendy departed for England with the children, taking what the papers would later euphemistically call a "holiday." During her time in the spotlight, she — in typically British fashion — remained tight-lipped about her feelings on Foikis' new vocation, although she did eventually admit to a *New York Times* journalist that there was "a period of adjustment."

Then, she added: "It was pretty rough for a while."

"The word I would use is: 'long-suffering,'" Annie Kitaeff said, of Wendy. "I always thought that at the time. Although his wife had made his costume for him, his first costume, I always wondered about her reaction to having a husband who was making being a fool his life's work. I think that must have been difficult for her."

But whatever his problems at home, out on the streets of Vancouver, his reputation was growing.

"Going with him, I noticed how many people knew and loved him," wrote journalist Richard Needham, "and how easily he got into conversation with everybody. But then, why shouldn't he?"

And as his confidence grew, he engaged in bigger and bolder acts of folly. On April 6, 1967, he was stopped by police as he tried to hand grape juice to Tom Campbell, while the mayor was busy serving the 1,000-person crowd pieces of a seven-foot birthday cake. And two months later, he made his first appearance in the newspaper — a short profile written by junior journalist Kathy Tait. By this point, he was a fixture on the courthouse steps and had gained enough of a reputation that, in early June, he wrote to city council, requesting an annual salary of $4,000. The money, he noted, would be easy to raise.

"A simple tax is all I need," he explained. "One cent per ordinary citizen, two cents per politician, and three for lawyers."

But his official "coming out" wasn't until the Canadian Centennial celebration, held in the courthouse square during July of 1967. By then, Wendy and the children were deeply ensconced in their English holiday, and as he always did, Joachim Foikis made his way to the courthouse square. Despite a clear blue sky, the day was an unseasonably cool twenty-one degrees, with winds of up to twenty miles per hour, but this did little to keep throngs of people from swarming into the downtown core. Bumper-to-bumper traffic filled streets across the province. There were fireworks, parades, and a one-hundred-round fire barrage at Brockton Point, courtesy of the 50th Field Artillery Regiment. At the nearby PNE Grounds, 30,000 people attended a 3.5-hour show recreating moments from Canadian history (with, *The Province* noted, "a strong military flavour").

Of course, not everyone was celebrating; the evening also featured a stirring statement from Chief Dan George, who chided the incredulous, 29,000-person crowd for its shameful treatment of Canada's Indigenous Peoples, citing in particular "fire-water and reserves."

"My people will not thank you for these things," George said, "but we should forget what is past. We want to join with the white man and look to the future."

Back at the courthouse, the festivities continued well into the evening, featuring dancing, music from a band called The Painted Ship, and serious technical difficulties, courtesy of Mayor Tom Campbell. After arriving late for his speech (leaving the crowd in silence for almost twenty minutes), he struggled to illuminate the four sixty-foot lighting towers assembled for the occasion.

"This is no way to start a second century," he grumbled.

In spite of the crowd, police reported no incidents throughout the day — which isn't to say there weren't any; while wandering the courthouse square, Foikis encountered a sailor on leave and had to scurry for cover when the sailor, believing he was a communist, pulled a knife. Hostile seamen notwithstanding, Foikis' reputation quickly grew from local to national in the weeks following the Centennial. Not long afterward, he was profiled by *The Globe and Mail* journalist Richard Needham, in whose columns he would make regular appearances throughout the 60s. By August, he had a spread in *Maclean's*.

Joachim Foikis instructs schoolchildren in the nature of folly, 1968

"The hardest people to get through to are the tense middle-aged businessmen scurrying from liquid lunches to afternoon bull sessions," wrote journalists Fred Haake and David Nybakken. "'I'm your looking glass,' the Fool tells them. 'Laugh at me and laugh in return at yourself.'"

But by the time Haake and Nybakken were trailing Foikis on his afternoon wanderings, his approach was starting to work — not just amongst the counterculture, but amongst that same contingent of businesspeople who had, until recently, looked upon him with contempt.

"Let's trade costumes," one businessman said to Foikis. "I've been a fool all my life."

"But," Haake wrote, "the real moment of triumph for Foikis came when a tired-looking executive spent his entire lunch hour studying the Fool's frolics intently. Finally, he walked over with a beam on his face and said: 'You're absolutely right. I'm taking the afternoon off.'"

Unsurprisingly, he was also a big hit with children, usually providing them with nursery rhymes or riddles.

"Who can put Humpty Dumpty together again?" he would ask. "That is the most important riddle in the world."

"Who are you?" asked a child one afternoon, as Haake and Nybakken watched.

"I am Jack the Giant Killer," Foikis replied. "The giant I kill is littleness — little hearts, little minds, and big chicken livers."

"There was the element of being on a spiritual quest and putting other people on the spot in the way that a guru might," said Annie Kitaeff, "although he didn't think of himself in that way. I think he thought of himself as maybe a portal, a gateway through which others could begin to look at themselves more deeply. For him, I think it was an interesting combination of the political and the spiritual."

Foikis, it seems, tended to agree with her assessment.

"Instead of becoming a preacher, I became a fool," he said. "There isn't much difference."

But at the same time, he emphasized the importance of spiritual philosophy, as a bulwark against the dehumanizing values of the modern world.

"There's a tremendous meaninglessness and loneliness which engulfs so many in Western society," he told a *Globe and Mail* journalist. "The meditative way of life has been completely suppressed since the Middle Ages. Unless people learn to meditate and contemplate again, and learn to find resources in themselves, they are going to be in a very bad state when the time comes that they are not fully needed in the production process."

For most of 1967, he confined the bulk of his activities to the courthouse square, sometimes moving through the streets — asking questions and dispensing nonsense. Sometimes, people started arguments, wanting answers, or demanding he account for his behaviour, but Foikis never took the bait.

"I'm a non-authority," he would claim. "I don't want followers. I don't present a doctrine or a dogma — only images. I don't approach anybody. I don't pester anybody."

But by the end of the year, he had started to — expanding his scope beyond the courthouse, to bring his "happenings" into people's homes and businesses. In October of 1967, he crashed a lunch meeting of the Optimist Club, sending attendees back to work "impressed but a little confused."

"As a fool, I confront people whose objective is to rise in the community," he told the crowd, "rather than to have a more abundant, fulfilled life."

"He's certainly not a crackpot," an attendee admitted to *The Province*. "He has set himself up in opposition to the establishment. I feel he's quite justified."

On the surface, his confidence in this topsy-turvy worldview seemed unshakeable. But privately, he had his moments of doubt — in his mission, in himself, and in the visions that had led him to this point (later in life, he wondered aloud to longtime friend Laurence Fisher whether it may have been "because he smoked too much hash or something").

"I sound so cocksure when I talk about reality and illusion," he mused. "But at heart, who can be cocksure about these ultimate things? My vision was so fantastic, but I worry sometimes that it could be an illusion. The reality of most people is an illusion. My revelation was only a glimpse of reality, but I'm still a fool."

And by November of 1967, he was something else: broke. City council had rejected his bid for a salary. In the nine months since he quit school, he'd survived on his savings, bringing in a pair of hippie boarders during the summer to help with rent. But as winter approached, and with his family back under one roof, he had no choice but to trade his motley for a set of coveralls, taking a job as a labourer with the Vancouver Park Board. But he was by no means hanging up his mantle for good; into the New Year, he split his time evenly between the park and the bauble, clearing trails three days a week in a pair of coveralls he had painted for the job — half red and half blue.

"The men I work with are very tolerant of my dress," he wrote, in a letter to Richard Needham, "and so are the supervisors. They're a good bunch. For me, it's presently a holiday from talking, and a time of preparation for a more effective way to spread joy and confusion."

As it turns out, the holiday would be a necessary one, and his money problems would soon be a thing of the past. Because, in just a few months, Joachim Foikis would become official.

5.

THE GRANT

"Any fool and his family can live on $200 a month. It's a veritable fool's paradise."

— **Joachim Foikis, *The Globe and Mail*, April 6, 1968**

IT WAS 1968, and Joachim Foikis was at the end of the road.

The savings he had been living on since the spring of 1967 were exhausted, and his attempt to get a grant from the city had failed. He had advocates on his side — in particular, journalists like Richard Needham and UBC professor and *Saturday Night* writer William Nicholls — who had started a "Save the Fool" campaign to raise money and book speaking engagements on his behalf.

"His message clearly is that we can abandon all the competitive games we play to become secure and rich, and that if we do, we shall find a way to happiness by simply being ourselves," Nicholls wrote, in a January 1968 *Saturday Night* article. "He thinks that many others could live a mythical role like his own and find a rich meaning quite different from those of the occupations our kind of society offers. To be a fool in the eyes of our kind of society may be the best way to find the wisdom of the poor in spirit. When we see that we are indeed completely ridiculous, we shall begin to see straight."

The previous October, while still clearing trails with the Vancouver Park Board, he had made mention of applying for a Canada Council grant, but there were few who had noticed the claim, and even fewer who had taken it seriously. But Foikis already had his eye on those in power.

"Who are the giants of this world?" he scoffed. "Those with tiny hearts, tiny minds, and big chicken livers."

Near the end of the month, he was declared official mayor of the City Government, a satirical organization set up by fellow academic and activist Stan Persky. Foikis accepted the post, and then immediately resigned, saying: "Only a fool would take on this job." In early April, his usual headquarters in the courthouse square briefly came under siege when Persky and several other youths were jailed for loitering. When Persky refused to post a peace bond, Foikis and representatives from hippie weekly *The Georgia Straight* headed to the city jail to cause a scene.

And then, on April Fool's Day, he got the news of a lifetime; the Canada Council for the Arts had approved his application, granting him $3,500 — more money than he had made annually for the past seven years — to embark on his mission. Many were flabbergasted at the news — not just that he had succeeded, but that he had applied at all.

"To be a rebel, you have to do your homework," he'd once said. "I study until 2:00 a.m. every morning. Mostly Shakespeare and Mother Goose."

To maximize his public exposure, Foikis chose to appear in the lobby at City Hall, where he was greeted by a throng of reporters. After answering their questions, he took time to thank the "three wise men" who had served as the council's judges: theatre critic James

Barber, UBC Religious Studies department head William Nicholls (who had also begun the "Save the Fool" campaign), and UBC fine arts professor Herbert Gilbert. Broadly speaking, there was enthusiastic support for the grant amongst business leaders (including the GM of the BC Tourist Bureau and the president of the Downtown Vancouver Business Improvement Association), as well as in the pages of the local papers, and even the BC Legislature.

Joachim Foikis, 1968. Image Courtesy of *The Ubyssey*

"We should do more of that sort of thing," East Vancouver MLA Alex MacDonald cheered. "It would inject a little fun and entertainment into our life."

Of course, not everyone was a fan.

"We have to get by on $1,200 a year," griped Vincent Yates, president of the BC Old Age Pensioners' Organization. "He's too damn lazy to get a job and do some work."

And lawyer Peter deVooght took his anger one step further, drafting a writ of prohibition to prevent Foikis from claiming the money at all.

"May I say at once I take strong objections to the grant. It represents squandering of funds belonging to the citizens of this country," he wrote, in a letter to council. "In the light of the strained economic position of the federal government and the crushing demands on taxpayers, the grant is no more than an incredible exercise of irresponsibility."

"I love seeing Foikis running around making an ass of himself," he added, in the pages of *The Province*, "but I'm not prepared to support him financially. There are too many real problems in this country that need public funds."

And the public, deVooght claimed, was overwhelmingly on his side.

"People have been honking their car horns, stopping their cars, waving and shouting to me," he continued. "The people I meet are jubilant, even some of the old age pensioners."

Despite the outrage, Foikis considered it a relatively moderate reaction.

"The greatest European town fool was hanged by the town fathers for upsetting the applecart," he pointed out. "If I had received a grant to catch butterflies at the North Pole, nobody would be offended, but I am being paid to prick the ego bubbles of the town's philistines."

When pressed for a response to deVooght's attempt to part him with his money, he replied: "It's a belated April Fool's Day joke, perhaps," before reciting a poem intended for the lawyer's ears:

> *"Oh, that I were where I would be,*
> *Then I would be where I am not.*
> *But where I am, there I must be,*
> *And where I would be, I cannot."*

For the remainder of the week, debates over the grant were held in the pages of the local dailies — in articles and in letters to the editor. Then, on April 2, Foikis responded to Tom Campbell's very public declaration of animosity, when a photograph of him thumbing his nose at the mayor appeared in the pages of the *Vancouver Sun*.

"Most people on city council are real estate moles who have their heads stuck in the ground and no vision," Foikis snorted. "Tourism isn't my aim, but I am of more value to Vancouver than $4,000 worth of tourist billboards. The people of Vancouver need the sort of thing that I am doing so that they will awaken from their sleep and arise from the dead."

Several tense days followed, but in the end, deVooght's attempts to interfere were unsuccessful. Joachim Foikis was now on the payroll as Vancouver's official town fool, the first to hold such a position in centuries.

"Of course, the charge that the fool is lazy and does no work is totally false and is based on a misconception as to the nature of work," an editorial in the *Vancouver Sun* argued, in support of his mission. "The fundamental objection to the fool goes far deeper than the charge (which we have seen to be erroneous) that he does no work. It is based on an unreasoning fear and hatred of anyone who dares to ridicule our obsession with material goals. We tolerate — even encourage — people who speak scornfully of God or religion, or Canada, or love, but let someone poke fun at money and our penchant for status-seeking, and the cry immediately goes up [...] Unlike the hippies, whom he superficially resembles, the fool stands for imaginative involvement in the problems confronting society."

"The trouble with many people is that they can never reach a threshold for what they think are their needs," Foikis told the *Vancouver Sun* shortly thereafter. "They keep escalating their needs up and up, and they can't keep up with them. I don't want to spend more time than necessary making money. I want the freedom to study and philosophize."

Now he could do both. He had succeeded in becoming Vancouver's official fool, but along the way, thanks to the efforts of men like Needham and Nicholls, his purview had expanded well beyond the courthouse square. Now, he was a fool with a national platform.

Joachim Foikis wasn't at the end of the road after all; in fact, he was just getting started.

9.

GREAT FALL (Part One)

"Two fools under one roof will seldom do any good."

— German proverb

THE FAIRY TALE WAS OVER.

Nonetheless, on April 29, two days after the money ran out, Joachim Foikis went to city council with a request: $4,000.04 — a fool's annual salary, just slightly more than the Canada Council grant, plus four cents for an alderman, he said, that he "considers a fool four times over."

Unsurprisingly, they weren't amenable.

"Any vote is a negative vote," Tom Campbell told *The Province*. In the hospital undergoing surgery, the mayor still managed to find the time to make his feelings known. "But if I were there, I would still vote in the negative," he added. "Any man who would waste $3,500 of Canada Council money…"

Unfortunately, the once benevolent Canada Council was another dead end; new chairman John Prentice had a less frivolous view of art and culture, one incompatible with the aims of men like Foikis. In the meantime, longtime friend Carey Linde and UBC professor Warren Stevenson had formed SPOOF — the Society for the Protection of Official Fools — in an attempt to raise money, soliciting donations in the pages of the *Vancouver Sun* and *The Province*.

"We in SPOOF believe Foikis has been a creative force in the city and at both universities," Stevenson wrote, "and that he is worth his weight in gold."

The Georgia Straight too waded into the fray, forming the Fool Tax Benefit.

In the meantime, Foikis had been on the road; in March, he was in Salmon Arm, using his Canada Council money to bid on hair clippings from the head of Kamloops Mayor Peter Wing, as part of a fundraiser for a boy who had lost his legs in a car accident. A few weeks before that, he stopped in Parksville to give a talk at a local coffee shop — one sponsored by the Parksville-Qualicum branch of the Voice of Women. There, with his young son Martin on his knee, he passed around tambourines and led a boisterous jam that delighted the young and irritated the old.

"Too many people are hung up on the idea of a guaranteed annual wage," he told the crowd, "and it's important to learn how to use leisure time, as automation will cut down work so much in the future that leisure will probably dominate."

When asked by a TV news crew about his own money problems — now growing more dire by the day — he seemed nonchalant, stating that he intended to continue as Vancouver's town fool, grant or no grant.

"He hopes to carry on with the help of welfare," the Nanaimo news media reported, "and is not concerned about lack of funds."

"In time," he said cryptically, "the unicorn will rule over the lion."

The Voice of Women seemed pleased with Foikis' talk, but there were many who found the experience unsettling.

"Reaction to his remarks was mixed," the *Nanaimo Daily News* wrote. "Some of the young people said they were inspired, while others were not impressed, and some adults said afterwards they feel that the type of advice given might be detrimental to young people."

In fact, this seems to have been the consensus throughout the spring of 1969: that Foikis' views — once considered charming — were becoming too extreme. Some even began to feel as though he had come unhinged. By now, he had also begun to resemble the hippies he had once kept at a distance; his hair was long and tangled. A wispy beard grew from his chin. His motley was falling apart; the cap was often nowhere to be found, and his bauble had been damaged beyond repair and eventually abandoned. His attacks on education continued; in March, he told a public meeting at Point Grey Secondary that school was a "a waste of time" and that the building's doors should be locked forever.

"A couple of people almost had a heart attack after some of his comments," reported an observer, in the pages of *The Province*.

And in April, he made a contentious speech in front of a standing-room-only crowd at the YMCA. While he had long maintained in the media that "I get high on Mother Goose, not drugs," he had since become a passionate advocate for the use of both psychedelics and marijuana — something that ruffled more than a few feathers.

"Marijuana is the gift of Mother Earth," he said. "After so many centuries of deadening our minds by rationalizing, the world needs the magic of total involvement. Young people are going to keep taking drugs even if you do put them in jail. Your culture is dying. We are giving birth to another."

Furthermore, he argued, the older generation would be even better served by psychedelic drug use, likening it to the magic mushrooms used in indigenous cultures for generations.

"You should be in jail!" shouted a disgruntled member of the audience. "You advocate marijuana so you can weaken a girl's resistance and take advantage of her."

"Do you think it would be more decent to use alcohol?" Foikis shot back.

"How about working for a living?" shouted another.

And, if the audience thought his views on drug use were extreme, his comments on marriage must have seemed stranger still.

"No marriage should last more than eight years," he told the crowd. "Every man should have two wives, and every wife should have two husbands. If there are new loves, there should be new marriages. There is no reason to kick anyone out. Just expand the tribe."

The crowd was incredulous.

"What if everyone was like you?" someone shouted.

Foikis smiled. "Life would be heaven."

The public disagreed.

In fact, their appetite for his foolery was swiftly waning; by May, SPOOF had collected just $100 of the $4,000 they wanted. And his money problems only compounded; by July, he was being sued for nonpayment of his Canada student loan — close to $2,000, including interest. His beloved Peter and Pan were trapped in impound. Later that month, he hitchhiked to Toronto for a court appearance, where he was fined $25 for shouting insults at a police officer. When he began playing his flute, the prosecution tried to get him removed for contempt of court. During his time in Ontario, he attended a "be-in," and subsequently held a "happening" on Parliament Hill, continuing his now-standard practice of passing out instruments.

"We are trying to stimulate the community," he told the press, "and a community only exists if people get together in the streets."

"Musical, however, would be the last word to describe the happening," noted the *Ottawa Citizen*, "which consisted of a small band of semi-dressed individuals tootling, pounding, strumming, and blowing on an assortment of instruments."

When he returned to Vancouver at the beginning of August, he was virtually penniless, surviving mostly on handouts and communal living situations.

"I have no money," he told *The Province*. "I'm completely broke."

Wendy and the children had applied for welfare, he noted, having just received their first food vouchers. Without money to free them, Peter and Pan were headed for the auction block. But even in such a dire situation, Foikis himself was adamant that he wouldn't take welfare money.

"I'll survive on handouts or sleeping in ditches and eating restaurant leftovers," he said. "I will try to keep on going even if my wife now calls me a creative bum."

This proved to be something of an understatement; it turns out the public weren't the only ones running out of patience.

"No marriage should last longer than eight years," Foikis had recently told his audience at the YMCA.

And his didn't. Before the summer ended, Wendy packed her things and vacated the little house on West Fifteenth, leaving for England and taking the children with her. Whether it was his constant absences, his views on marriage and fidelity, or his lack of income is difficult to say.

"She was very tolerant for years," Foikis admitted later. "Her dreams of a house in Kits went down the drain. Finally, she couldn't handle it."

Over the next six years, he would see his wife and daughter only sporadically. After 1975, he wouldn't see them at all.

His last meaningful appearance in a major newspaper took place near the end of December 1969. And the man profiled was a very different Joachim Foikis. His hair was even longer than before, his beard bushy. His glasses were gone, his motley replaced by jeans and a ratty-looking rabbit-fur coat, recently donated by a friend. In photographs, the mischief is gone from his eyes; instead, he glowers at the camera from a distance. When located by the *Vancouver Sun* journalist Neale Adams, he was sitting with a small group of friends in the Student Union Building, idly playing the flute. And when he spoke, it was in the mournful tone of a man who had lost everything.

"It's not the town fool anymore," he said, gesturing to the others. "It's the company of fools."

The "happenings," he said, were now smaller and more sporadic — usually at universities, usually in Ontario.

"Sometimes they pay me and sometimes not," he explained. "They have to pay my way there since I have no money."

He made no mention of his wife and children. Instead, he emphasized his desire "to try the poverty trip." On Saturday nights, he noted, he and the group would visit local restaurants, collecting waste and leftovers, to use as food for the week.

"They're happy to see us," he told Adams. "Otherwise they'd have to throw the food away."

His plans for the future were nebulous, though the "company of fools," he noted, would likely use Vancouver as a home base to travel throughout BC and Canada. But he quickly grew weary with Adams and his questions, instead pivoting to talk of environmental degradation.

"Your papers just tell about the bad things, the bad trips," he complained. "You should have left up those ten trees or however many it was that the paper was made out of. They were alive. The newspaper is death."

Then, he got to his feet.

"I don't want to talk," he said flatly. "This interview isn't what I'm about. Come and see me, and we'll go and have a happening."

He had always been a man on the outside, and now, he was drifting even further out to the fringes. But his peers too had moved on; the City Government was dead. Stan Persky had left town. The hippies had established communes in the Fraser Valley or cut their hair and gotten jobs. *The Georgia Straight* become little more than a repository for advertisements and adult personals. In 1972, even Tom Campbell didn't run for re-election.

"My next step is to move away from this world and into another world," Foikis once told a reporter. "Out of our world and out of your world and into another world."

"He just said, 'I'm not going to be shackled by any obligations to anybody,'" friend Carey Linde later added. "The state, income tax. Anybody."

As the 1960s drew to a close, it was unclear what the future held. Whether the fool would return, triumphant, as he had pledged before the coffee shop crowd in Parksville. Whether he would head up the company of fools, travelling the country, as he'd claimed to Neale Adams. Then, sometime in early 1970, Joachim Foikis boarded a plane to Europe, for a rare family visit. And during the flight, he had another of his mystic experiences. But this time, it wasn't a vision. It wasn't an angel. It wasn't a moment of transcendence or chaos. It was a feeling of loss. The departure of something inside that he hadn't noticed until it was gone.

In time, perhaps, his prophecy would come true. In time, perhaps, the unicorn would rule over the lion. But not today. Today, the fairy tale was over.

Once, years ago, he had left his native Europe to find the end of the world.

Now, the end of the world had found him.

FOOL'S PARADISE

"I throw my bauble in the air all the time. Once in a while, it falls on the ground. The bauble falls on the ground all the time, but I don't think the clown on the bauble is upset about it. Like the bauble, I don't get upset by living in this fallen world."

— Joachim Foikis, 1968

2.

END OF THE WORLD

"Some fools seek wisdom high and higher,
To MA, PhD aspire,
Though people deem them very bright,
These fools can't understand aright."

— Sebastian Brant, *Ship of Fools*, 1494

IT WAS 1955, and a twenty-four-year-old Joachim Foikis had just arrived in Toronto, looking to start over. Outside of an accounting career, he had no firm plans upon his arrival, and before long, he decided that the city didn't agree with him.

"I regard Toronto as a frightening vision," he later told a journalist, "a vast complex of grey and black buildings."

So, on a whim, after just a year and a half, he jumped on a bus and headed west.

"I don't know why," he shrugged, "except that Vancouver is the end of the world. I got on a bus to the end of the world, and I found this."

What he found was the University of British Columbia — that, and a woman named Wendy Cossins. Like Foikis, she hailed from abroad — Somerset, England — and the pair met over the course of 1958 while Cossins worked as a dietician at Vancouver General Hospital, and Foikis was studying social work at UBC — the first of several degrees he would earn over the next decade. Inside of three years, they were married, and settling down in a house on fifteenth avenue in nearby Point Grey.

"It is like a fairy tale," Foikis later mused. "The prince went to the end of the world and he found the princess."

When discussing his life, he would often refer to it as "the fairy tale," although Wendy may not have seen it that way; early in their courtship, Foikis took a job as a counsellor at the nearby Haney Correctional Institution, but like his tenure in Toronto, it didn't last. By 1960, Wendy was supporting them both, something she would continue to do for several years while Foikis wandered from degree to degree — from social work, to theology, to library science. Although, as he later pointed out, by the time they were married, the future Wendy Foikis would have harboured few illusions about her future husband.

"When I married my wife, I promised only that she would never have a Cadillac or a mink coat," he told a reporter. "I have never cared about rising in the world. I have no desire to be successful in social terms."

Despite the unusual vows, their wedding went ahead in 1961, and the following April, Wendy gave birth to their first daughter: Karen Elizabeth Foikis. Shortly afterward, Foikis graduated with a degree in social work — he appears, looking clean-cut and studious in the 1962 alumni handbook *The Totem* — and almost immediately, Wendy became pregnant again. But before the family could properly settle into their quiet, new routine — child-rearing, work, and study — tragedy struck.

It's likely that, shortly after they brought Karen home, they noticed something was wrong. Perhaps it was fatigue. Perhaps it was a fever that never seemed to go away. Possibly, it was pallor or shortness of breath. In any event, they brought their daughter back to the hospital she had just recently left, and the diagnosis was devastating: leukemia. This news was paramount to a death sentence; today, thanks to advances in treatment, recovery from childhood leukemia is almost a foregone conclusion, but in the early 1960s, Karen Fojkis' chances of survival were zero. In mid-November, she was admitted to the pediatric ward at Vancouver General Hospital, and placed under the care of Dr A.F. Hardyment. And it's extremely likely the family rang in 1963 at her bedside; on the 2nd of January, Karen died, at just a year and eight months old. Her body was cremated two days later.

It's impossible to know for certain what effect this had on their new family. She was never mentioned in interviews, never spoken of by any friends or acquaintances. But the psychological impact of losing a child is always profound, plunging grieving parents into bouts of depression, anxiety, marital strife. The lingering effects of such a loss can last for years, leading to PTSD, and even suicidal urges and reduced lifespan. It's also impossible to know what effect this event had on the path Joachim Foikis chose to take. Was his descent into folly a way of reverting to childhood, to avoid the guilt of such a crushing parental failure? Or had it triggered an existential crisis that made him re-examine his priorities?

At first, it seems they tried to put the incident behind them. In short order they moved into a new house, getting a sweetheart of a deal on a small, white bungalow on West 13th Ave — just $75 per month. In the fall, Foikis again enrolled at UBC, this time studying theology. In any event, as their home life descended into madness, so too did the world around them. An American president was killed in Dallas. His successor joked with reporters about the size of his member while simultaneously ordering the bombing of innocent

civilians in Vietnam. Youth counterculture exploded, with some —
like Ken Kesey and his Merry Pranksters — inadvertently following
in the footsteps of the Elizabethan fools as they travelled across the
country in a modified school bus, with heads full of LSD and an
ethos that was equal parts protest and performance art. North
American society was in the midst of a seismic cultural shift — one
that had begun with the Beat Generation, and evolved to encompass
art, music, academia, and politics.

In 1965, as the family welcomed another daughter, Rebecca, Joachim Foikis made two choices that would turn out to be fateful
ones: first, he applied for a Canada student loan in the amount of
$1800. Second, he enrolled in a 400-level Buddhism course taught
by a UBC professor named Arthur Link. As the fall semester began,
and the Foikis family wrestled with their grief, the streets of Vancouver suddenly seemed like a place where a fool lurked around
every corner. It was a world in serious need of a skewering. All
around, values were begging to be upended. Egos bubbles were begging to be pricked.

But the Fool of Joy was dead. There was no Will Sommers with
his incisive wit, no Diogenes with his lantern, no Till Eulenspiegel to
speak truth to power. Long ago, the bauble had been dropped, and
despite the desperate need for a social critic, for a looking glass, no
one had picked it up again.

That was about to change.

11.

"MEANINGFUL WORK"

"And what is all this life but a kind of comedy, wherein men walk up and down in one another's disguises and act their respective parts, till the property-man brings them back to the attiring house."

— **Desiderius Erasmus, *In Praise of Folly***

IT'S FITTING THAT KATHY TAIT, who wrote the first newspaper profile of Foikis, also wrote the last.

Tait had been the one, as a junior reporter, to tell her peers of the fool's existence, after running into him on the courthouse steps during a lunch break back in the spring of 1967. And in 1999 — thirty-three years after her first story — Tait managed to track him down in Esquimalt, where the sixty-four-year-old was living in a studio apartment, getting by on his old age pension and the proceeds from bottles he collected in Victoria's Inner Harbour. He was still an avid gardener, tending a plot at a nearby lodge, and another at a community garden. He also had several flats of tomatoes growing in his apartment. His life was simple; he spent his days conversing with friends at a coffee shop on Government Street. He was missing many of his teeth. He wore a sweater he'd found in an apartment disposal chute. He made art from scavenged materials — including wood and broken tiles. He hadn't spoken to his wife or daughter since 1975. Rebecca had since become a computer engineer in England, likely settling in Manchester. His son Martin — with whom he still spoke — was working as an instructor at York University.

"I sure missed them when I lost them," he said.

Joachim Foikis in Victoria, 1999.
Image Courtesy of Postmedia, *Vancouver Province* Archives

Before his arrival on Vancouver Island, Foikis had spent years living in an SRO hotel near the Carnegie Public Library at Main and Hastings Streets, in the heart of the Downtown Eastside. Though his locale had changed since the 60s, his priorities had remained the same: he spent the bulk of his time at the library reading or in conversation on the streets with friends, strangers, and anyone in between. On one occasion, he visited the library's special collections to demand his clippings file, but otherwise, he kept out of the spotlight; his only newspaper appearance during those years was in the "Help Wanted" section, where he offered "intelligence, maturity, honesty. Desire meaningful work. Kim Foikis. 321-3218."

"He just lived a simple life," explained former neighbour Cindy Taylor. "He was extremely intelligent, but he just wanted to live a very simple life."

Several times over the course of the early 1990s, Taylor visited him in his room near Main and Hastings Streets, catching up and talking about old times. Carey Linde, too, paid him a visit — but found himself deeply concerned by the changes in his old friend.

"He was living down on 'Skid Row' for some time," Linde recalled. "He was mad at that point — in the sense that he was really into a whole bunch of stuff, which made perfect sense on an intellectual level. He was absolutely right with his critiques and his understanding of what was happening, but his efforts … I don't know."

Linde and Taylor both lost touch with him after that; during this period, Foikis' mother — one of the few family members with whom he still had any kind of relationship — passed away, and he used a portion of her estate to move to Vancouver Island. And there, it seems, "meaningful work" found him — or something close to it. Moving into a communal house in Esquimalt, he took a job as a clerk with the Ministry of Environment, gaining access to slews of maps for regions all over the province.

"I remember one day, a package showed up in the mail, and it was from Kim," Cindy Taylor said.

Inside was a provincial survey map of the property they had shared on Lasqueti. It was the last contact the two would ever have. And during his final interview with Kathy Tait, the environment seems to have become his main focus, even outside of work.

"It was great fun," he told Tait, of his years of folly, but "it's trivial, compared to the fact that we are trashing the planet for the sake of the stock market."

He had often spoken out about environmental causes during his fool period (in part, Peter and Pan were a comment on auto emissions), but those concerns had grown considerably in the ensuing years, and now his assessments bordered on apocalyptic.

"Mother Earth," he said, "is growing impatient."

Tait's profile — like others from that time — tended to paint the aging Foikis as a tragic figure. Friends spoke of him in similar tones; instead of a rising devil, he was a fallen angel — or, as in Linde's case, a madman. They wrote or spoke of his scavenged clothes, his meagre old age pension, his missing teeth. Someone tortured by what he had lost, someone driven into "self-imposed exile" by the ghosts of his past. A family abandoned, perhaps, or a young daughter lost. But Cindy Taylor saw it differently. She saw a man at peace. A man who sidestepped the narratives foisted upon him by others. A man not prone to madness or melancholy, who knew those narratives were just a reflection of the viewer's folly. A man on a singular quest that had begun during his high school days in Berlin, and who had found what he was looking for — first in books, then by reflecting it outward at the world — and finally being content to nurture it within himself. He'd found the truth. And the truth was simple.

"He didn't really change much over the years," she argued. "I don't know if he had any buried things that troubled him, but he just had such a simple life, and he expressed himself pretty honestly. I think whatever difficulties he might've had, he'd put them behind him."

8.

DRUM AND COLOURS

"A great while ago the world begun,
With hey, ho, the wind and the rain,
But that's all one, our play is done,
And we'll strive to please you every day."

— Feste, *Twelfth Night*

IT ENDED WITH A BANG.

It was 11:00 p.m. on a Saturday, in the spring of 1969. The intersection of Granville Street and Broadway. Revellers were filling the sidewalk, fresh from a lecture/meditation session with famed Buddhist philosopher Alan Watts. Many carried instruments — Watts had requested musical accompaniment for the evening, and his audience eagerly obliged, bringing along flutes, cymbals, and tambourines. The energy on the sidewalk was infectious, and within a few minutes, more than 200 people had crowded together. And in the centre of the crowd, pounding his drum in rhythm, was Joachim Foikis.

He'd been less visible during the spring of 1969, splitting his time between Vancouver and Toronto, and during that period, he seems to have found his groove. After a year on the road, he had grown tired of talking about his position, preferring instead to spend time creating street "happenings" that brought together people, music, and dancing — happenings that encouraged community and joyful, reckless abandon.

As Foikis shouted and beat his drum, the crowd began to dance. Cymbals crashed. Flutes trilled. A circle formed, with Foikis and four men seated on cushions in the centre, leading the music. By now, the crowd was so large that it spilled into the road, snarling traffic for blocks and eliciting angry honks from passing motorists. Things became so boisterous that an irate neighbour called the police, and in short order, Constable David Athans and Corporal Don Keith were dispatched to the scene. When they arrived, the party was still going; Foikis' voice could be heard shouting "Om" over the roar of the crowd, urging them to keep dancing. Athans and Keith pushed their way into the cacophony of crashing cymbals and banging drums. Upon seeing the officers, Foikis was unconcerned, inviting them to "dance and have fun."

"I told him I didn't want to dance and asked him to come with me," Athans later testified.

BANG went the drums.

"What's this all about?" Athans asked.

"It's not about anything," Foikis replied. "It's just having fun."

BANG. Foikis turned away, pounding his drum, urging people to keep dancing.

"The streets are for people," he added, "and there's nothing wrong with that."

BANG. Furious, Keith grabbed Foikis by the arm.

"Stop making those noises," he shouted.

Foikis smiled and beat his drum. "You mean these noises?"

BANG. BANG.

By this point, Keith had had enough; he grabbed Foikis and tossed him into the back of a waiting police van. But the crowd wouldn't allow it; they rushed forward, cutting Keith and Athans off from the van. A woman ran up to Foikis and tried to kiss him. Even after the police got him into the back of the van, the crowd surrounded it and tried to pry the doors open.

"Who's in charge here?" Foikis winked. "The police or the people?"

He was no more contrite when he appeared in court several days later, in front of Magistrate Morris Mulligan, on charges of disturbing the peace; when asked to justify his actions, he picked up the Bible and quoted Psalm 150: "Praise him with the sound of the trumpet…praise him with stringed instruments and organs." During the proceedings, Foikis conducted his own defence and called his own witnesses. Despite this open defiance, Mulligan dropped the charges — although he also seems to have missed the point.

"There's a time and place for most things," he concluded. "I don't think the corner of Granville and Broadway between 10:00 and 11:00 at night is the right time or the right place for this thing of yours. But on the whole of the evidence, I must dismiss the charge, and you are free to go."

This wasn't the end of Foikis' legal troubles. At the end of March, he would again be arrested for disturbing the peace — this time while beating a drum outside Yorkville Avenue's Penny Farthing coffee house — in front of a crowd of hundreds. This time, he was jailed overnight, and when he appeared the next day in court, he received a stern rebuke from Judge Michael Cloney.

"We don't need any court jesters here," Cloney barked. "You behave yourself as people should behave themselves in court."

"We should behave like human beings," Foikis replied.

Then he started juggling an orange. An outraged Cloney threw him in a cell for a further two hours, before ultimately releasing him on $100 bail. Foikis remained in Ontario for several more days, choosing to spend April Fool's Day on Parliament Hill, where he intended to pay a visit to the offices of the Canada Council. He didn't even make it through the front door. Before going inside, he taped a small sign to the main door of the centre block, one that quoted Marshall McLuhan.

"The young will continue turning on no matter how many of them are turned off into prisons," it read, "and such legal restrictions only reflect the cultural aggression and revenge of a dying culture against its successor."

Security was furious. One tore the sign down and shouted at Foikis to "go back where you came from."

"I said I would be up," he later told a reporter, "but the guards wouldn't even let me in. I was so put off by the treatment I received at the parliament buildings that I left for Montréal."

By this point, his weariness was evident. And with good reason; his home life was in shambles. He was in constant trouble with the law. His donkeys kept being impounded. SPOOF was sputtering. The public seemed to be tiring of his antics. Creditors were at his door. And just $500 of his grant remained. There was a good chance that, inside of a month, his time as Vancouver's official fool would be over. But rather than vanish into obscurity, using the last of his funds to stave off poverty for a few more weeks, he decided he wanted to go out with a bang.

"I want to revive the Fool of Joy," he once told a reporter. "I want all the world to be a stage — and get every other fool to laugh in the face of death."

And so he did, making one final, public statement — about community, about folly, and about basic humanity.

Foikis rose early on the morning of April 27, 1969. It was a Sunday, sunny and unseasonably warm. He dressed in his motley, slung a large bag over his shoulder, and stepped outside. By 9:00 a.m., the neighbourhood children had already begun to talk. Foikis was on the sidewalk, they said. And he had instruments. He had gone to a local music store and spent what was left of his grant on percussion instruments and noisemakers — hundreds of them. Now, he was giving them away. But the children of his neighbourhood weren't his goal. Instead, he lugged his sack of instruments onto a downtown bus and headed for Pigeon Park, in the heart of the Downtown Eastside.

"A fool's music broke the drab routine of Vancouver's Skid Road Sunday," wrote Kathy Tait, in the pages of the *Vancouver Sun*, as Foikis began handing instruments to those seated in the park. Many of them were low-income residents of the nearby hotels, most struggling with mental health and substance issues. He passed out instruments — flutes, drums, and cymbals — as well as flowers and food. Then, as always, he began to beat his drum.

BANG.

BANG.

BANG.

The crowd began to grow, with others grabbing instruments of their own and adding to the noise. Soon there were more than two hundred people, dancing, singing, laughing, putting daffodils in their hair.

BANG.

BANG.

BANG.

A small group of Indigenous women began to move and chant in unison, in what the paper mischaracterized as a "sun dance."

"They have not had so much fun in the last twenty years," a grinning police constable told Tait, while stationed nearby.

Among the audience that day was UBC fine arts professor Herbert Gilbert. Gilbert was one of the Canada Council judges who had awarded Foikis his grant, and he was impressed by what he saw.

"Foikis has sparked a vitality where everything else has failed," he said to Tait, mesmerized. "I have travelled around the world, but nowhere have I found this kind of an atmosphere. It's like something you would expect in Tangier or Istanbul, but it's right here in Vancouver."

BANG went the drums. The steady heartbeat of a community united.

BANG.

"He has planted the seeds of a relaxed humanism," Gilbert beamed. "He has peeled off the masks of fear. He's done something to get people mixing together as human beings."

And it worked. The Sunday "happenings" would continue into the summer, steadily growing in size with each passing week. They were a place of joy, of connection, of community. A stage. A place to laugh in the face of death. Thanks to Joachim Foikis, the streets were once again for people — but not just the affluent or the privileged. Not just men like Tom Campbell or Peter deVooght.

They were for everyone.

For a brief period of time, he had succeeded in bringing people out of their shells and helped them find expression and freedom, just as he had once found them himself.

"It was something to get outside myself," he told a *Vancouver Sun* reporter back in 1968. "I was too introverted. But now I have met so many people. And I have helped quite a few in their folly, I think."

But even then, he knew the end would come. He spoke of it often. Recognized it. Relished it. And the end, he knew, would bring with it a different kind of freedom.

BANG.

BANG.

BANG.

Into the distance. Into an uncertain future. Each movement throwing off the weight of years.

"I hope someday a better fool will come along," he said, to director Tom Shandel in 1968, "who will take over the bauble and wield it better and more effectively. Then I can go back to my books in my home, and take off this costume and burn it, and be on my own, and have my freedom completely."

There is one surviving photo of the Pigeon Park street party; it's of Joachim Foikis, surrounded by revellers. His beard is unkempt and his hair shaggy. His fool's motley is barely visible beneath his coat. He has a drum in one hand and a flute between his lips. And in his eyes — as always — is a hint of mischief. Mischief, and what looks like pride. For a few short minutes, in a small corner of the world, he had his freedom completely.

BANG. BANG. BANG went the drum.

He grinned. Then he took a bow and left the stage.

FOOLS RUSH IN

An edited conversation between Vancouver's town fool, Joachim Foikis, and *The Ubyssey*'s Arnold Saba (March 29, 1968)

FOIKIS: We are all looking for a medium in which to communicate. People are finding it worthwhile to communicate something that they believe in. And the question is, what do you want to communicate, in what form, in what manner? You can teach, or write, or paint, or you can live your words. In a way, that is what I am doing. I go out in the streets. I am relating my vision in images, which may even be perceptible to those who are illiterate. Not those that can't write or read, but those that can't see, they are also illiterate.

SABA: Do you claim to have a vision?

FOIKIS: I say you live in a world of unreality, and I believe that whether you call it a vision or what, I've stepped into reality, and I'm presenting reality in the disguise of a mask, the fool, which is assumed, and I am an actor on the stage.

SABA: Do you feel you are getting through now?

FOIKIS: Well, even while I am getting through, there is the danger of becoming entertainment, rather than communicating subliminally. Entertainment helps to sustain people in the cave in which they find themselves, the grey world of everyday existence. Plato says only a fool wants to remain in the cave when the light is to be found outside. But the cave is secure, while outside is dangerous. It's a matter of not having faith, and not having a clear enough vision.

SABA: Is it ever possible to get through to the majority of people?

FOIKIS: Well, I don't worry about that. I don't believe in elitism, which says the kingdom is for the few, not for the many. Who is the devil? The man of expediency. The man who is essentially blind. I represent — through the medium of the stage — man's vice, his folly, his inability to see clearly. Harlequin is one of the seven devils. He belongs to underground religion. The overground religion, the Billy Graham type of religion, the nice clean boys, proclaim happiness as a result of negation. Religion has done a complete switch. The underground religion thinks highly of myth, not law or literacy. The best way of passing on a vision is mythology. This is where the churches are breaking down.

SABA: Don't you think man's situation has always been negative? Because the same religion has always arisen.

FOIKIS: But the religion has always lost its vision or something. The more sensitive people in the last few hundred years have become dissatisfied with the completely puritanical, unenlightened vision. The orthodox and the money-makers go hand in hand, you know. Two bad visions. Two bad trips, both.

There is a complete topsy-turviness of appearance and reality. Here is this idea I use of the fall of the world. It's Humpty Dumpty. The cosmic egg becomes fragmented, the Hump is the heaven, the Dump is the earth, the egg yolk is the sun, and all the other parts are the cosmos.

SABA: Would you class yourself as wiser or more foolish than the establishment?

FOIKIS: I would consider myself a bit of a lesser fool. Maybe this is arrogance, but I've got the licence to be arrogant, because I personify the cock.

> *The cock doth crow*
> *To let you know*
> *If you be wise*
> *'Tis time to rise.*

I feel I am happier and more controlled in what I am doing. You've got to listen to the person whose message reflects his experience, not his reading, not somebody else's authority. He whose message and life are identical will carry a little more power than those whose life and message are completely at odds. Like Billy Graham.

SABA: What about the straight people? You can't dislike them.

FOIKIS: You want to turn them on. You want other people to participate in the dance of life. The most effective way is like a pyramid — you want to be at the top of all the dead bodies. But when you invert the pyramid, like the Canadian pavilion at Expo, at the bottom is the fool, and the other people dance just as high as they can. This is the vision of non-competitiveness in a social structure. You want the other person to dance higher, because he will carry you along. But if you don't pull the others up first, you will just be supporting their weight all the time, all the dead bodies, and who can live among the dead?

Kids today want to get out of their home situation, because they can see clearer the essential hell.

SABA: You seem to feel we're heading towards some sort of apocalypse.

FOIKIS: Well, we are still playing the game, but under very absurd and laughable conditions.

SABA: Is man holy and profane?

FOIKIS: Yes, surely they belong together, the spirit and the body.

SABA: So you don't believe in the devil as in Milton.

FOIKIS: No, I believe in the devil as in Shakespeare. In *Twelfth Night* the devil is Malvolio, the man of ill-will, the Puritan, the man of expediency. [. . .] The Puritan fights his own devil and becomes completely obsessed, and separates from God that way, from the light [. . .] The devil is not an immoral devil, but a blind devil. The devil is folly. The moral trip is an irrelevant trip.

Oh, I should not be doing so much analysing. I should just spout nursery rhymes. I have a more effective medium than analysing. I believe in myth, and myth is a representation of psychic reality, in its purer forms. It doesn't demand intellectual affirmation but presents the same reality in a simpler form. I don't want to pass on information. I want to create images, or maybe that's another way of passing on information.

I only wish that other kids would find their medium, which I've been looking for for such a bloody long time, so they could join in the fool's comedy.

> *Good times ahead*
> *Awake all sleepers and rise from the dead*
> *There are good times ahead.*

The world is governed by folly. Well-being is it. Just contribute your own little brick. Every fool according to his own talents . . . dum dum dum . . . that's all you are requested to do. You don't have to do any toil. It's a Divine Comedy. Maybe you're still waiting for Godot, the Little Prince. But you know he is coming. You don't have to ask if he exists.

ACKNOWLEDGEMENTS

First off, I want to extend my heartfelt thanks to Carey Linde, Laurence Fisher, Cindy Taylor, Stan Persky, and Rick and Annie Kitaeff; without your insight and your stories, I would have had nothing. Thanks to *Superfool* director Tom Shandel for allowing me to see Kim Foikis goof around and swing on swings, and to hear him speak in his own voice.

As always, to Brian and Karen at Anvil Press for the opportunity to explore weird local lore — and for their infinite patience (especially since this time it was more infinite than usual). Thanks to Lani Russwurm for being awesome enough to keep splitting that Newspapers.com subscription. Thanks to the family — Mom, Dad, Caley, Kirsten, Coda, Monty, and Abbey — for being the best, kindest, funniest folks a neurotic weirdo like me could ask for. And of course, thanks to Jess; my love, you're the one I want to watch the ship go down with.

And finally — Rebecca and Martin: I tried to find you. Lordy, I tried. I combed through marriage records and faculty directories and emailed a whole lot of people I've never met. If you're out there, and you're reading this, I hope I didn't fuck it up too badly. And if you have anything to add, for good or ill, please get in touch.

I'd love for us to help each other fill in the blanks.

Material on pages 52 and 98 republished with the express permission of: *Vancouver Province / Vancouver Sun*, a division of Postmedia Network Inc.

NOTES

April Fool's Day

The quote about Foikis "radiating life" comes from Nancy Beckett, in the September 12, 1967 issue of the *Globe and Mail*.

Foikis' story about the angel and the bauble is taken from the July 25, 1967 edition of the *Vancouver Sun*.

His remarks at city hall were reported in the April 2, 1968 issue of the Vancouver *Province*, and his comments about the Fool of Joy are taken from a March 2, 1968 profile in the *Globe and Mail*.

Foikis' question: "Are you a man or are you a fool?" is taken from multiple newspaper sources, as well as interviews conducted by the author with Rick & Annie Kitaeff and Stan Persky.

Mayor Campbell's comments about seeing red appeared in the April 3, 1968 issue of *The Province*.

1: FOLLY OF YOUTH

Foikis' quote about the history of the Silesia region comes from a profile in the July 25, 1967 edition of the *Vancouver Sun*.

Relevant information on the history of European fools, the quote from Frederick I, and the story of the Berlin cabaret comedians are taken from Beatrice K. Otto's book *Fools Are Everywhere: The Court Jester Around the World* (University of Chicago Press, 2001).

The quote about Nasrudin's "divine madness" comes from "The Turkish Jester or The Pleasantries of Cogia Nasr Eddin Effendi" (Nasreddin Hoca, 1884).

Joachim Foikis' quote about fools and puritans, and his description of his first vision are both taken from the July 25, 1967 edition of the *Vancouver Sun*.

The description of his early life comes from the May 14, 1968 edition of the *New York Times*.

The dates of Foikis' time in the Hitler Youth are taken from an interview that appeared in the May 15, 1968 issue of the *Billings Gazette*.

Foikis' quotes about the Hitler youth and the SS are both taken from the November 14, 1999 edition of the Vancouver *Province*, and his quote about Grimm's Fairy Tales comes from the April 27, 1996 edition of the *Vancouver Sun*.

Information on the Free University of Berlin is taken from Udi Greenberg's "Germany's Postwar Re-Education and Its Weimar Intellectual Roots," *Journal of Contemporary History* Vol. 46, No. 1 (January 2011), pp. 10-32

2: END OF THE WORLD

Details about Vancouver during the 1960s is taken in part from Lawrence Aronsen's *City of Love and Revolution* (New Star Books, 2010), as well as from the recollections of Rick and Annie Kitaeff, Stan Persky, Carey Linde, and numerous contemporaneous newspaper sources.

Foikis' quote about Vancouver being the end of the world, and his thoughts on Wendy and material things are both taken from the July 25, 1967 issue of the *Vancouver Sun*.

Mayor Tom Campbell's grumblings about Kitsilano hippies comes from
the March 8, 1967 issue of the *Vancouver Sun*.

Harold Kidd's interview about the hippie invasion of Kitsilano comes from
the August 7, 1968 issue of the *Vancouver Province*.

3: EPIPHANY

Carey Linde's recollections are taken from an interview between Linde and
the author, fall 2019.

4: VALENTINE'S DAY

Joachim Foikis' quote about seeing the archetypal fool comes from the May
13, 1968 issue of the *New York Times*.

Remarks about his "fantastic vision," inverting the social order, and "joyful
symmetry" are taken from the 1968 CBC documentary short *Superfool*,
directed by Tom Shandel.

Wendy Foikis' reservations, and the quote about roaring "off to town to buy
material for his costume" is taken from a profile of her in the March 1, 1968
edition of *The Province*.

The approximate date of Foikis quitting university, and his comments on
hippies both come from a profile in the July 25, 1967 edition of the
Vancouver Sun.

Foikis' admission that he was less than forthcoming with his wife is taken
from Kathy Tait's November 14, 1999 retrospective in *The Province*.

His comments about being an introverted bookworm are taken from the
March 2, 1968 edition of the *Globe and Mail*.

The use of the word "holiday" to describe Wendy Foikis' escape to England
also comes from the July 25, 1967 issue of the *Vancouver Sun*.

Wendy's comments about the strain on her marriage are taken from the
May 14, 1968 issue of the *New York Times*.

Richard Needham's quote about Foikis, as well as Foikis' quip about the fool and the law come from the September 1, 1967 issue of the *Globe and Mail.*

His first appearance in a newspaper is a profile by Kathy Tait in the June 7, 1967 issue of *The Province,* and news of his letter to council appears in the June 9 issue.

Reporting on the Fool's interactions with downtown businessmen is taken from the August 1967 issue of *MacLean's.*

Foikis' discussion of meditation and the Middle Ages is taken from an interview in the *Globe and Mail,* October 17, 1967.

His "happening" at the Optimist's Club, and all related quotes, are from the October 19, 1967 issue of *The Province.*

Foikis' comment about smoking too much hash was taken from an interview between the author and Laurence Fisher, fall 2019. His quote about being "cocksure" is from Tom Shandel's film *Superfool.*

5: THE GRANT

Foikis' remarks about reviving the fool of joy come from the March 2, 1968 issue of the *Globe and Mail.*

His quote about rebels doing their homework comes from a profile in the July 25, 1967 edition of the *Vancouver Sun.*

Peter de Vooght's comments, and his letter to council are explored in the April 4, 1968 issues of *The Province*, and the *Nanaimo Daily News.*

Foikis's story about the hanging of the European town fool is taken from the *Vancovuer Sun*, April 3, 1968, and his riddle comes from the April 4 issue.

6: FOOL ON THE HILL

Foikis' quote about Humpty Dumpty comes from an article in the *Globe and Mail*, September 1, 1967.

Jack Mangles' financial offer was reported in the April 10, 1968 issue of the *Vancouver Sun*.

Foikis' quotes about Ontario and Toronto are taken from the May 10, 1968 issue of *The Province*.

His quote about being an apprentice is taken from the March 28, 1968 issue of the *Globe and Mail*.

Foikis' quote about Mayor Dennison lacking imagination comes from the May 21, 1968, edition of *The Province*.

The *Take Thirty* interview with Joachim and Wendy Foikis aired on June 28, 1968.

Foikis' trip to Essalen, and his comments about making street theatre are chronicled in the June 18, 1968 issue of *The Province*

Foikis' interview with the *Battle Creek Inquirer* is taken from the November 24, 1968 issue.

Tom Shandel's recollection of *Superfool* comes from an email exchange between him an the author, August 2020.

Bob Hunter's story about Joachim Foikis and his musical instruments comes from the May 22, 1969 issue of the *Vancouver Sun*, and is described as having taken place "last winter."

7: PETER AND PAN

Information about Foikis' car crash, and Wendy's quote about searching for donkeys both come from *The Province,* April 18, 1969.

The scene with the donkeys at city hall is taken from the May 10, 1969 issues of the *Vancouver Sun* and *The Province*.

The various escapes of Peter and Pan can be found in the May 22, May 27, June 21, and August 14, 1969 issues of *The Province*.

The auction is recounted in detail in the August 22, 1969 issue of *The Province*.

9: GREAT FALL (PART I)

Joachim Foikis' trip to council chambers, and all related quotes, is reported in the April 30, 1969 issue of *The Province*.

Tom Cambell's reaction comes from *The Province,* April 29, 1969.

SPOOF's fundraising efforts can be found in the *Province*, May 17, 1969.

His adventure to Salmon Arm is chronicled in the *Province*, March 3, 1969, and his trip to Parksville appears in the *Nanaimo Daily News*, February 28, 1969.

His comments on education appeared in *The Province*, March 6, 1969.

SPOOF's fundraising failures, and Foikis' YMCA talk are both detailed in *The Province*, May 27, 1969.

The musical happening on Parliament Hill appears in the *Ottawa Citizen*, July 14, 1969.

Foikis' final interview of the 1960s appears in the December 17, 1969 edition of the *Vancouver Sun*.

10: MAGIC MOUNTAIN

Laurence Fisher's recollections come from an interview between Fisher and the author, 2019.

Joachim Foikis' quote to Kathy Tait about the end of his fool period comes from a November 14, 1999 retrospective in *The Province*.

Rochdale College's mission statement is taken from the *Toronto Star*, February 6, 1968.

Historian Stuart Henderson's quote about Rochdale comes from the *Globe and Mail,* November 8, 2013.

The quote about the evictions come from the *Toronto Star*, May 30, 1975.

Jim Washington's quote about his education at Rochdale is taken from the *Toronto Star,* June 7, 1975.

The Toronto Star's erroneous story about Foikis and his wife comes from the May 4, 1972 issue.

The Earthling Survival Society's call for a new fool was reported in the *Hartford Courant*, November 5, 1974.

Doug Hamilton's quote about Lasqueti, and much of the contextual information on the island in the 1970s is taken from *Accidental Eden* (Darlene Kay Olesko and Douglas L. Hamilton, Catlin Press, 2014).

11: "MEANINGFUL WORK"
Much of the relevant information for this section is taken from Kathy Tait's retrospective in the November 14, 1999 issue of *The Province*.

12: GREAT FALL (PART II)
Details of Joachim Foikis' death come from the June 8, 2008 issue of the *Globe and Mail*.

Information about the Arizona high school student's plunge into the Inner Harbour comes from the April 3, 2007 issue of the *Victoria Times-Colonist*.

About the Author

JESSE DONALDSON is an author and journalist whose work has appeared in *VICE*, *The Tyee*, *The Calgary Herald*, the *WestEnder*, the *Vancouver Courier*, and many other places. His first book, *This Day In Vancouver*, was a finalist for the Bill Duthie Booksellers' Choice Award (BC Book Prizes). His most recent book, *Land of Destiny: A History of Vancouver Real Estate* was a BC Bestseller. He currently lives near Mount Pleasant with Abbey, the world's best dog.